THE DEATH EXPERIENCE:
What it is like when you die

Richard Brannon:
The Afterlife is Real.
Enjoy The read!
Alan Ross Hugenot

By Alan Ross Hugenot

info@afterlife.pro

First published by Dog Ear Publishing
4010 W. 86th Street, Ste H
Indianapolis, IN 46268
www.dogearpublishing.net

ISBN: 978-1-4575-1334-3

This book is printed on acid-free paper.

Printed in the United States of America

*"What is REAL?" asked the rabbit one day, when they were
lying side by side near the nursery fender, before Nana came
to tidy the room."*

The Velveteen Rabbit, by Margery Williams 1922,

*"If a man dies shall he live again? All the days of my appointed
time will I wait, till my change comes"*

Job 14:14 (NIV)

*"All come from dust and to dust all return. Who knows if the
spirit of a man rises upward…"*

Ecclesiastes 3:20-21 (NIV)

*"Mankind's spiritual future is a grander field of inquiry than
the principles of mechanics"*

Edward C. Randall, c.1906

ABSTRACT:

This is a book about the current science of what happens just after you die

INTRODUCTION & HOW TO USE THIS BOOK: Provides the setting, describes the history of the science, and explains how best to view this material

PART 1 - THE SCIENTIFIC BASIS and SOME NEGLECTED HISTORY: Examines and analyzes the latest supporting evidence for consciousness survival, including; studies on remembered past lives at University of Virginia, After-Death communications at University of Arizona (Veritas graduate studies program), Near-Death experiences (NDE) by the *International Association for Near-Death studies* (IANDS), and collates this with recent consciousness research including, mind over matter (psychokinesis) at Princeton University, and remote viewing (clairvoyance) studies at Stanford Research Institute. I also describe my own first hand experience of the other side during an NDE.

This evidence is collated with what is currently postulated regarding the non-physical dimensions of consciousness as supported by quantum mathematics, string theory, M-theory, de-coherence and quantum resonance, the Zero Point field and the now postulated Quantum hologram.

The consciousness survival paradigm which all this points to, is then compared with the after death beliefs of the world's current religions and also with the ancient Egyptian afterlife myth which included karma and reincarnation and which substantially agrees with what current science has found. This includes the belief by the early Christians in karma and reincarnation and then reviews the history of the government mandated changes in Western religious beliefs enforced under penalty of death by the Roman emperors in the 5th and 6th centuries, which imposed the myth of the *single lifetime*, which now dominates Western culture

PART 2 – THE ROAD MAP: Provides a description of the death process and what you will experience as the physical body shuts down and your consciousness makes its transition to the alternative reality of the afterlife. This is based on first-hand experiences of 20th and 21st century Near-Death survivors, which has been carefully collated with the ancient records regarding the death process, in *Tibetan Book of the dead* and the *Egyptian Book of the Dead*.

TABLE OF CONTENTS

PART 1
THE SCIENTIFIC BASIS and SOME NEGLECTED HISTORY:

PART 2
THE ROAD MAP

CHAPTER 1

INTRODUCTION

"I would like to suggest that superstition is very simple:
it is merely belief without any evidence."

Carl Sagan, Gifford Lecture No. 1, 1985[1]

"Now faith is the substance of things hoped for, the evi-
dence of things not seen".

The Bible, Hebrews 11:1 (KJV)

Superstition is not very scientific, yet both traditional religions and the materialist science community base their chosen beliefs about the afterlife entirely on superstition, since neither offers any evidence or proof for their belief system (B.S.).

Although, we have known the methods of modern scientific inquiry since Newton (1642-1727), until now, no one has bothered to use rigorous science on the question of the afterlife. One early afterlife researcher summarized this problem succinctly:

"In the long story of man's endeavors to understand his own environ-
ment..... there is one gap or omission so singular that its simple state-
ment has the air of paradox. Yet, it is strictly true to say that man has
never applied the methods of modern science to the problem which
most profoundly concerns him——whether or not his personality
involves any elements which survive bodily death."

Fredric W. H. Myers in 1901.

Consequently, this lack of reliable information has forced society to rely instead on a great deal of speculation and superstition. For example;

- **Religious people** *hope* **that there is a life after death,** which they want to believe "by faith" in their chosen scriptures (Bible, Quran, etc.) rather than by scientific proof. But, if *belief without evidence* is in fact superstition, as Carl Sagan proposed, and if *"faith is the substance of*

1

things hoped for the evidence of things not seen", then saying they prefer "faith" is the same as saying they prefer superstition over facts.

- **Scientifically inclined materialists, on the other hand,** *want* to believe that there is nothing besides physical matter which could possibly survive after death of the physical body. Yet, they have no proof whatsoever for the underlying premise that, "material matter is all there is in the universe". This bed rock belief is actually an unproven and unsupported superstition of the 19th century. But, in the 20th century quantum mathematics, non-locality and Heisenberg's uncertainty principle have completely falsified this archaic materialist belief.

Also, in the last 50 years several prestigious universities have sponsored rigorous scientific research into several independent disciplines, which all now point to the same reality of consciousness survival in an alternative dimension. This alternative paradigm correlates findings of research being conducted on:

1. The Near-Death experience (NDE),
2. Children who remember prior lives (CRPL),
3. Adult past life memories (APLM), and
4. After-Death communications (ADC), and
5. Physics of quantum mind and conscious will in quantum mathematics.

This book is about that alternative paradigm regarding what happens after your consciousness leaves your physical body. This paradigm is **neither religious nor materialist**, but is instead based on implications of quantum mathematics and the Near-Death experience.

SO, WHAT EXACTLY HAPPENS AFTER YOU DIE:

Some people worry that death will be painful, and others believe it will be more like, "the lights suddenly going out and never coming back on". Instead, research shows that death could better be described as:

> **"Lifting a curtain and moving on into the next stage of the continuing existence of your consciousness".**

Not surprisingly, the Spiritualist movement has been saying something very similar since the middle 19th century, but with insufficient rigorous and replicated science to back up their beliefs.

However now in the 21st century, the inclusion of conscious will into sub-atomic particle science of quantum mathematics, coupled with extensive study of the Near-Death experience, have verified what mediums have been describing about after death communications since biblical times and also collated well with what the ancient Egyptians and Tibetan Buddhists have been saying for several thousand years about repeated lifetimes, namely......

"There is no death, there are no dead"

Instead, the collected evidence when taken altogether provides replication of the fact that the individual consciousness does survive physical death.

> *"We now have, for the first time in the history of our species, compelling empirical evidence for belief in some form of personal survival after death."*
> Robert Almeder, ©1992 Ph.D. Professor of philosophy,
> Georgia State University.

HAVING A ROAD MAP:

When planning a trip to an unknown country, tourists access travel guides written by someone who has been there and who can tell them what to expect. Likewise, this book collates the experiences of those who have traveled to that *unknown country* on the other side of death, and provides a reliable road map of the death process as experienced by many persons, including the author, who have previously died. It also describes what your upcoming journey will be like and what you can expect as you move beyond this physical life.

SCIENTIFICALLY VERIFIED TRUTHS: What is presented here contains no unsupported superstitions derived from ancient religious scripture or out dated Newtonian science. Instead, it is based on the collated first-hand experiences of people who have actually died and come back to life, and is also extensively compared with the rigorous and replicated science which backs up their documented experiences.

OVER 100 YEARS OF COLLATED RESEARCH: Modern medicine's ability to keep us alive has greatly increased the rate of occurrence of the phenomenon called the Near-Death experience (NDE). There are now thousands of people who have died and were later brought back to life, who have been describing an alternative existence beyond physical death. Their reports, which are collected and collated over the last 30 years by the *International Association for Near Death Studies* (IANDS), agree with what other unrelated research has been finding since the late 1960's through the study of thousands of cases of children who remember prior lives (CRPL). Each of these remembered past lives has been thoroughly investigated and the details of the remembered prior lives verified by the *University of Virginia*. Also, the Spiritualist movement has been verifying consciousness survival through After-Death communications (ADC) since 1848, as have also the British *Society for Psychical Research* (SPR) since 1882, and the *American Society for Psychical Research* (ASPR) since 1884 and Gary Swartz Ph.D & Julie Beischel, Ph.D at the *University of Arizona* have also been investigating ADC through the *Veritas* graduate program which concluded in 2008. All of this independent evidence, when taken together, replicates the conclusion that consciousness survival is a fact.

AN ANCIENT GNOSIS: This alternative paradigm has now been established as a scientific fact and is not merely some "New Age" belief system. Historical research has found written accounts of the dying process, which precisely parallel the NDE, dating back several thousand years to the very beginning of writing. Even Plato describes a Near-Death experience as early as 450 BC.

Further, accounts of Near-Death experiences and After-Death communications also appear in the Bible. So, when a religious leader smugly says, "The church does not believe in the Near-Death experience", the underlying truth, of which he/she is unaware, is instead that, *"The church no longer chooses to believe in reincarnation or the Near-Death experience,* but, this has only been true since Emperor Justinian's politically inspired rejection of reincarnation in 553 AD. Prior to that edict, the early Christian fathers believed in reincarnation and the Near-Death experience. For example, the revered Christian St. Paul describes his own NDE in Second Corinthians 12:2-6 in the Bible, and the Christian Bishop Origen of Alexandria (184-253AD) clearly believed in karma and reincarnation. Further, that revered Doctor of the Christian Faith, Saint Augustine, describes several NDE's in his writings some 120 years before emperor Justinian officially outlawed such beliefs,

The pre-Christian ancients also recorded their knowledge of the death process in several ancient texts including:
* The Tibetan Book of the Dead, and
* The Egyptian Book of the Dead

I examine here the agreement of these ancient beliefs about death, carefully comparing and collating that consensus with the modern NDE and recorded details of the death process, which different mediums have received from an individual surviving consciousness, and find them all to coincide with the NDE.

"*The hardest thing was to get rid of the blood*", Bob said, "*the ceiling of the master bathroom was a blue enamel, and when we first painted it with latex the water in the latex soaked up into the floor boards and loosened up the dried blood in the wood fibers (which had been there over 90 years), the blood colored the latex with a stain. Eventually, we had to remove the latex, paint over it with an oil based product to contain the blood stain, and then etch the surface with an acid and repaint with the latex, just to get the white ceiling you have been seeing in there*".

As he took his leave he said "*Again, please keep this quiet so as not to disturb the other guests*".

That night there was no sign of Charlie and we left the following morning.

After we returned home, I asked the Pastor of my Lutheran congregation in Seattle, what the church said about Ghosts. He told me that the church does not have any precise doctrine on Ghosts. He said that he personally felt the often reported phenomena of Ghosts might actually be, "*souls of persons who had not yet discovered that they were dead*". But, he cautioned me that anything else the church might come up with was strictly speculation, and that they carefully avoided creating a doctrine about this.

On the other hand, the Hasidic Jews have been studying this phenomena and working on this doctrine for several hundred years and have formulated some fairly firm conclusions. Here is what Rabbi Yonssan Gershom said in his 1992 book,[52] where he says that there do appear to be some common factors that hold spirits earthbound.......falling into three main categories:

1. **The spirit does not know that it is dead:** While it may seem incredible that someone could die and not realize it, this does happen. Such a soul often has no belief in life after death, and therefore reasons that, because it still has consciousness it cannot really be dead. Also if the death happens suddenly, the transition to the afterlife can be so fast that the soul does not realize it has taken place.

   Note: My own personal NDE (1970) left me with memories of waking up with the light, but never passing through a tunnel or leaving the body (I definitely remember returning back into the body) but I had no memory of my actual death. Consequently, I can understand that a surviving consciousness could be dead and not realize it.

2. **The soul has stereotyped expectations of the next world:** Many people simply do not realize that all religious descriptions of the afterlife are only metaphors or speculations, and when they die they expect their beliefs to be fulfilled literally. For example, the absence of a Heaven with angels plucking harps, may cause some Christian souls to remain earth bound because they will not accept the help of the spirits who have come to meet them. And in some cases may believe that the helping spirits are demons in disguise, just because that is what they were taught to expect by their overly confident preachers who are so sure their ancient speculations are correct.

    Also, Edward C. Randall (1906) assisted numerous earthbound souls to move on during his years working with Mrs. French. He says that half of every evenings sessions for over 15 years were devoted entirely to this "mission work", assisting earthbound spirits to move on towards the light, and in several cases there were Christians literally, as Rabbi Gershom said, waiting for the savior to show up and believing that the spirits of their dead relatives were imposters.[53]

3. **The soul has unfinished business**: This is the most difficult type of earthbound spirit to work with, because in order for a soul to be released into the light it must want to go. As long as it feels that it has not completed its work here on earth, the soul will continue to be attached to persons, places, or things in the material world.

    Note: This is the reason that most Near-Death experiencers return to their physical bodies, they had unfinished business, here in the physical which they return to complete before finally moving on.

At the time, although I knew from my own NDE that the afterlife existed. I also knew that during out of body experiences NDE participants had always found it impossible to communicate directly with the living. So I had assumed until then that it was not possible for a disincarnate consciousness to communicate with those still living in the physical, and also that After-Death communication must simply be imagined. Consequently, what I had experienced at Crockett Farm was something that,

"I would not have believed if I hadn't personally been through it".

In fact, if Anna had not told me about her dream *before* breakfast and prior to hearing Bob's stories, then I would not have been *left by the circumstances with no choice but to believe it.* Fortunately, the sequence of events left me no explanation other than that it was actually some form of valid After-Death communication (ADC) phenomena. It was obvious that Anna knew parts of the story of Charlie's murder (which occurred 90 years earlier in that house), and she knew it before anyone told her about it. Further, she told me the details of what she had seen in her dream before anyone had told either of us about the events in that house.......

For me, *this again changed everything*. ....Plausible deniability was no longer one of my options......... I now knew that at least some form of communication from the Afterlife directly from disincarnate spirits to ordinary individuals was valid.

The result was that this unplanned episode, forced my mind into contemplation on the issue of After-Death communications (ADC), and how that might relate to the things I had learned in the Near-Death experience. This gnosis began to accelerate me down the path of exploration which I had begun with my NDE.

I realized at the time that either Anna was a deeply feeling person who could absorb the story through what I would later discover is called psychometry, or she had mediumistic abilities and Charlie's spirit was actually communicating with her.

At that time I began to conjecture that the violence in the hallway may have forever altered the energy of the house as stored in some universal recording device (Akashic Field), in such a way that she could still detect it 90 years later, something like a steadily playing video. After much additional research I would later allow the possibility that Anna might have established p-car resonance and quantum coherence with the DNA in the dried blood which had soaked into the floor/ceiling over the bathroom, and which contains the quantum hologram of the event which can be read magnetically similar to an fMRI scan.

On the other hand, and this still today seems the most plausible answer,.... it actually was Charlie's ghost (disincarnate consciousness) still living there and whispering in her ear using ESP and her intuition to send images into her head.

CENTURY OLD ADC VERIFIES MODERN NDE:

THE FRENCH REVELATION: In 1906, Edward C. Randall a well known New York lawyer published his findings after 15 years of research into after death communications (ADC) working with one medium, Emily S. French using the ADC phenomena called direct voice. Here is what he received from a deceased individual's surviving consciousness communicating to him through the mediumship of Mrs. French, nearly a century before the Near-Death experience was recognized as valid by the medical community.

Randall's reports have been researched and re-compiled by N. Riley Heagerty in a book entitled, The French Revelation ©*1995.*

DR. DAVID C. HOSSACK'S DEATH PROCESS[54] **as reported in 1906:** The following is a published description of the death process and awakening into the afterlife, as experienced and reported to Edward C. Randall by Dr. David C. Hossack who had died 60 years earlier. It clearly matches the events of the modern Near-Death experience, yet, this description came through during a séance in the years before 1906. Randall, had spent many years talking to disincarnate spirits from the other side while working in the presence of medium, Mrs. French. But, living in the late 19th century and early 20th century, he had no opportunity to have ever heard of the modern idea of the Near-Death experience, and at that time the ancient accounts of the NDE were obscure ancient literature. Yet, what Randall reports as being received from a surviving consciousness is *identical* to the NDE. Here is that description of the death process (*parenthesis are the authors comments*).

"There was this meeting and greeting with my own (family) who came to welcome me, as naturally as one returning after a long journey in the earth-life would be welcomed. Their bodies were not so dense as when they were inhabitants of earth, but they were like my own. Then I was told that my body and the bodies of all those in that life were actually the identical bodies that we had in earth life divested of the flesh covering. I was also told that the condition was a necessary precedent to entering the higher life, and that such bodies in earth life had a continuity and, further, that in leaving the old, I had come into a plane where all was etheric (dark energy), *that is matter vibrating in perfect accord with my spirit, technically speaking, the "etheric self"* (dark mater spirit body). *To me everything seemed perfectly natural to sense, sight, and touch.*

"Again, let me tell you, that the outer flesh garment is not sufficiently sensitive to feel, the etheric body (spiritual body) *alone has sensation.......I found little body change, I had sensations and vision and my personal appearance was in no way changed except that my body was less*

*dense, more transparent as it were, but the outline of my form was defi-
nite, my mind clear, the appearance of age gone, and I stood a man in
the fullness of my mentality, nothing gained or lost mentally.*

"What impressed me most after meeting with my own (family & friends)
*was the reality and tangibility of everything and everyone. All those with
whom I came in contact had bodies like my own, and I recognized friends
and acquaintances readily. Now, I will tell you of the one thing that
impressed me most on coming here. That was that matter in its intense
refinement, in its higher vibration (as observed here), was capable of
intelligent thinking and direction. Shape and grasp this proposition if
you can; I could not in the beginning, nor could I comprehend at once
that **all in the Universe was life and nothing else.***

> Here Hossack is stating a very Buddhist principle that earth, plants,
> insects, bacteria, animals and humans all are the same life, Think
> "Leaves of Grass" by Walt Whitman

"This fact, which we now know (in the afterlife)*,will overturn the
propositions of science (*in the physical life i.e. 3-D space-time*). "*

*"In all the orthodox teaching of nearly two thousand years, not one law
has been given tending to show how it was possible for individual life to
hold continuity. Theology had claimed it without explaining how or
where. This no longer satisfies the human heart or mind, a fact which
accounts for the great unrest amongst your people in every land. For this
reason it has been our aim to explain the law through which life is continued, and so simply to state the facts and explain the conditions that
all may understand. "*

*"**The key to comprehension is first to realize that your Earth** (reality as
you perceive it) **DOES NOT CONTAIN ALL THE MATTER OF THE
UNIVERSE, that all that you see and touch is but the substance used
by life in growth** (i.e. light energy).**

*When one leaves the earth-condition (*light energy*), divests himself of
the physical housing, he, through such change (*into dark energy*),
ceases to be mortal. By becoming a resident of the new sphere (*dark
energy*) he is said to take on immortality, but in reality, **he has always
been immortal.***

*"You regard the telephone as wonderful, wireless telegraphy (*radio*) more
wonderful still, but we communicate with each other by simple thought
projection (*ESP*). You regard the phonograph as a marvelous instru-
ment, but it is crude beside the instruments in use among us. When you
appreciate the truth that **we live in a state no less material that your
own** (*dark matter*), you will understand that with our greater age and
experience we are much in advance of you, and make and use appliances*

and instruments that could hardly be explained to mortal mind (which cannot yet even discern dark energy or dark matter). *At another time I may be permitted to discuss the subject more fully."*[55]

Note *In the bold text here, Dr. Hossack is talking about the quantum mechanics of string theory and alternative dimensions, which did not begin to enter modern physics until 30 years after Randall published this account of Hossack's revelations.*

SCIENTIFIC REPLICATION: For me, the fact that Randall, who at the time could know nothing about the Near-Death experience, was reporting this same phenomena in 1906, some 80 years before modern studies of Near Death Experiences began, provided effective replication through double blind conditions for purposes of comparison with the modern NDE.

A century earlier Randall delivers the same information which now occurs in all modern NDE's. This is compelling proof of two things:
- First, it is replication of my own experience, and
- Second this replication is virtual proof that Randall was actually communicating with a surviving consciousness on the other side, who had also been through the same death process as described by the NDE

The only difference between what Dr. Hossack experienced and what Near-Death survivors are reporting is that Dr. Hossack *did not come back to his prior life*, as all the NDE people have done. Instead Dr. Hossack is reporting the same after death experience while he is now a surviving consciousness in the afterlife. This amounts to scientific replication of my own experience which appears to prove two things:

1. The NDE is, in fact, the same process that is actually experienced at death.
2. Mediums do, in fact, communicate with disincarnate spirits (surviving consciousness).

The simple fact that a disincarnate surviving consciousness knew things about the death experience, and also about quantum physics and the conscious universe that Randall could not possibly have known in 1906 is strong evidence of the survival of Dr. Hossack's consciousness in a separate reality. This disincarnate consciousness communicating with Randall purported to be the surviving consciousness of the late Dr. David C. Hossack. My own research shows that Dr. Hossack was a former professor at Columbia University (King's College), and founder of the Columbia Medical School. Dr.

That night I woke in the middle of the night in an absolute fright (full adrenalin rush, heart pounding, breathing heavily). I immediately grabbed the pad of paper and wrote down the dream as follows:

> *I had been dreaming that both my parents had asked me to write a message in the snow so that it could be seen from any airplanes flying over. Apparently, we were stranded somewhere in the Canadian North beside a log cabin. It was terribly windy and well below freezing and I believe that I had been instructed to write out the words "Doubt not" so that the words would be visible from aloft. My deceased father (appearing very much alive) stood near a log cabin sheltered from the wind by the building and my mother (who was not yet deceased) sat silently on the cabin's small porch.*

> *They were both encouraging me to continue writing the message. I had formed the "D" with a trench in the snow. I had used a large empty tractor tire or inner tube to form the "O" and here is the scary part which awoke me mid-dream, they were encouraging me to cut up some small puppies with a chain saw, and use the bloody carcasses to form the letter "U".*

> *But, doing this awful deed of using a chain saw to slaughter living puppies was so against my nature, that I was becoming nauseated.....and despite their continued insistence,....... I refused to cut up the young living puppies with the chain saw.*

This attempt by them to require me to go against my nature and do something I saw as "not right" struck a very deep chord....... And I suddenly awoke without finishing the dream deeply shaken.

I almost never remember a dream, and my father has never appeared in any of my dreams before..... I got out of bed and wrote down the dream on the pad with my hands still shaking..... Slowly, I began to realize that the dream was exactly what I had prayed for and asked my father to do for me......, a dream from him that I could remember.

My intuition then gave me the following interpretation of what my father was communicating through this dream.

- First, he was continuing his previous message that I had received from him in a prior tarot reading. Which was that, "Death does not exist as we envision it", and that I should "DOUBT NOT" that the consciousness continues.
- Secondly, he was sending a second message in the form of a confession that he now realized that the forceful control, which he and my mother had tried to use upon me and my siblings, had been against my sensitive and feeling nature, and, that I was also correct in having resisted it.

- Finally, he had chosen this message of directing me to chop up puppies, specifically because it would shock me enough to cause me to wake up and so remember to write down what I dreamed.

The overriding message was his confession (and asking for my forgiveness) for having tried to break my sensitive nature. It was apparent to me that being on the other side he can see more clearly now than he could when he was here in the pain and emotions of the physical.

You can contact your deceased relatives in this same way. It just takes a strong belief that they can hear you and will also contact you, and being willing to face whatever comes with an open heart.

CHARLIE'S GHOST – Sometimes life leads us into events which provide a gnosis which we then can no longer deny. Such a personal encounter with an "earthbound" disincarnate consciousness unfolded in the fall of 1988 during a weekend stay at a bed & breakfast with my first wife, Anna. The encounter was entirely unexpected, but the facts surrounding the encounter made it completely undeniable showing me that After-Death communication is real. The week after it happened I wrote it up as the short story which follows.

The cold November wind blowing up from Admiralty Inlet skittered the dry leaves across the gravel parking lot as the November moon shown through forlorn tree branches surrounding the vintage house at Crockett Farm, a little bed and breakfast above Keystone Harbor on Whidbey Island, in Washington State.

Pebbles crunched in the chill as Anna and I approached the front door. We had come for a weekend to this pastoral retreat, hoping to re-kindle some romance after 17 years of married life. I had called ahead to tell the proprietor that we'd be arriving late after the other guests would have already retired. So he now quietly showed us to our room, whispering, "I'll show you the rest of the house tomorrow..... You're staying two nights anyway aren't you?

"Yes, see you in the morning for coffee", I whispered back, as we placed our luggage into the downstairs master bedroom just off the entry hall.

"Coffee in the Library at 7:30 to 8:30. Breakfast at 9 in the dining room", he said softly as I closed the door to our room.

Shortly, we retired to the Victorian quilts of the queen-sized bed. Anna slept near the bay window where the moonlight eerily sifting through the leafless branches moving in the night's offshore breeze. Repeatedly that night, I was re-awakened by Anna's tossing and turning.

After an imperfect rest, we awoke with the sunrise, and later, as I shaved and she worked with her curling iron in the shared bathroom mirror, she suddenly said, "I had the strangest dream last night. And, it kept waking me up,....... and then it kept returning when I got back to sleep......... I must have dreamed it four or five times."....

After years with her, I knew she was sensitive to subtle vibes, and could read people's feelings from across a room. She often had wild night visions that would portend coming events. So my interest was now heightened anticipating what she might now reveal.

"Well......" she said, "There were two elderly men running up and down the stairs in the hall,....... and they were shooting at each other with rifles, or long guns. ....But, they did not know we were here in the downstairs bedroom",... she said. .... "The continuing violence agitated me and woke me up, again and again........but, each time I fell back asleep, then they returned again with their guns".

"Strange that it kept coming back", I mused..... "Shall we get some coffee?"

In the library we met some of the other guests chatting amiably, and shortly, we were all seated in the dining room. After everyone had been served, Bob, the innkeeper began to tell us all about the house. He was an experienced story teller with a Masters in English Literature and held everyone's rapt attention.

> *"Colonel Walter Crockett was a Virginian who moved out here in 1852-53, along with the more famous Colonel Ebey, who homesteaded just to the north on Ebey Prairie. Crockett homesteaded the lands surrounding Crockett Lake. Colonel Ebey was killed by the Haida Indians in 1854 and they stole his head taking it with them back to the Queen Charlotte Islands (Haida Gwaii) off the west coast of British Columbia.*

He continued with interesting details of the local history until he came to the 1890's. when he said,

"Charlie Crockett, moved back into the farm house after he sold his home-stead to the U.S. Army Coastal Artillery so they could build Fort Casey on Admiralty Head, where you see the gun emplacements today......

I wondered about how much the government had to have paid Charlie Crockett to acquire the entire homestead as Bob continued his story.
"Colonel Crockett had left this farm house to his youngest son Walter Jr.... Apparently, neither son had ever married, and both were reclusive. Some folks said Charlie was actually an anti-social hermit type". The innkeeper continued.

"In 1896, a few years after Charlie had moved back in with Walter Jr., Charlie committed suicide shooting himself with a shotgun in the upstairs bedroom",

Suddenly, Anna jumped out of her chair, and screamed, *"No..., they shot at each other, both of them were running up and down the stairs..... I dreamed about it all last night !!!"*

The inn keeper's mouth fell open, and he stopped in mid-sentence............ Recovering, he said sternly, *"Ma'am, I don't want to hear any more about your dream".......*

With that he abruptly ended his tale. He excused himself and retired to the kitchen. He did not return to continue his narrative. Obviously, he was very upset by her response. The other guests hurriedly finished their breakfasts as an uncomfortable silence filled the room. Shortly they all left for their rooms.

Anna and I had drifted into the library without speaking......... "So much for a romantic weekend", I thought to myself,....... "Now she has gotten our host mad at us".

We refilled our coffee mugs and sat in silence looking at the shelved library books..... not speaking, we pretending to read........ The single night guests quietly checked out, paid their bills, and drove away leaving us in the great house alone with the proprietors.

"Oh there you are", said the inn keeper after the last guest had left. *"I must apologize for my stern reaction to your dream, and I must explain".*

"Truthfully, Charlie's death, was only listed as a suicide, which is also how I choose to tell the story, but it has always been suspected by all the local historians that it was really a murder.......

"The Sheriff did not declare him dead until 24 hours later, because his brother Walter Jr. did not report the death until the day after he died........ Charlie lay on the floor up there, while his blood ran down through the floorboards into the ceiling of the bathroom off the master bedroom where you are staying.

"So, when you spoke this morning, I was not at all mad at you. My ire was instead directed at Charlie, or his ghost. I got upset because we believed that we had previously exorcised his ghost out of the house. But apparently, he was still able to influence you. You are the first sign we've had of Charlie in over two and a half years.

"Because you are staying through tomorrow you might want to check out this whole story in the local cemetery, library and museum. Later, I'll tell you more, but please keep the "haunting" a secret. I advertise this place as a peaceful pastoral setting for a romantic retreat and not as a "haunted house".

Suddenly, the weekend had reversed itself again as we now had a detective adventure to pursue together. Now, we were involved in all the intrigue of a John Grissom novel.... Excitedly, we drove toward Coupeville in search of clues.

At the cemetery we discovered that Charlie was buried at the farthest end of the family plot, as if he had been disowned, but Walter Jr. was buried right up next to Mom and Dad.

At the museum we found odd references to the "suicide" often in quotation or parenthesis, as if it were actually not a suicide. We pieced together the story that apparently, the Sheriff had decided to declare it a suicide to avoid an expensive forensic investigation and trial. What would have been the point of convicting an elderly man to a life sentence when the criminal might die himself before the trial was even over. Instead of wasting tax payer's dollars, the Sherriff had simply declared it a "suicide".....Case closed.

In the late afternoon we returned to the farmhouse and the innkeeper, Bob, told us a great deal more about his own experience while we enjoyed the sunset across the inlet.

"We have been open three years now, but when I first bought the farm", Bob said, *"We had visions for a bed and breakfast much like you see today. But, on the first day we were here, while we were out chopping weeds, a neighbor came by and said, 'I see you bought the haunted house', at which point I knew we were in trouble"*.

"Since that time I have personally interviewed everyone who is still living who ever owned the house. Back in the 1970's the same psychic who had assisted the New York Police with the Son of Sam murderer, came and held a séance at the farmhouse. The psychic found that Charlie was killed rather than committing suicide, and apparently did not yet know that he was dead, which is why he hasn't yet moved on.

"A couple who owned the house sometime after that, and lived here for about ten years, said that on cold evenings, if there was a fire laid in the fireplace, Charlie would often light it while they were out watching the sunset. They also said that Charlie liked to close the library door, and would often wind clocks. Their mother-in-law once saw an apparition of Charlie in the Library and ran out of their house refusing to visit them again.

"All of the prior owners tell similar stories. So, we hired the Anglican Church to come and do an exorcism in each room of the house. And, since that time we have not seen any sign of Charlie in the house. At least, that is, not until this morning when Anna told us about her dream.

"The unsettling part of this is that, after I thought about it I realized that I never told you anything about the house, and never gave you a tour when you came in late, and neither did my wife. So, I was wondering just What did you know about Charlie before you came here?"

"We had never heard of him", I said, *"All we knew was that this was a peaceful pastoral place, and that it was a bed and breakfast on the island. We had never even heard of Colonel Crockett,... although I did know who Colonel Ebey was"*.

"Just as I supposed", he said. *"So, then this almost qualifies as an actual 'sighting"*, he mused, *"The first one since the exorcism. So, it appears Charlie is still here, we have just banished him from being inside the house, but he was still able to communicate with Anna through the bay window on the southeast of your room. It was fascinating how sure she was that it was a killing and not a suicide"*.

In this case there was no living person who knew the location of that will, or that it even existed. But, it was the deceased father's consciousness living in the afterlife, who wanted to set things right four years later. So from beyond the grave he took the effort necessary to communicate through a vivid dream to those still living. *You can verify this story by just Googling Chaffin's Will.*

3. GEORGE PELLEW'S ADC:[46] A very famous medium in New York City, Mrs. Piper, channeled the consciousness of George Pellew, who had died five years previously. Mr. Pellew spoke with over 150 different people who attended various séances conducted by Mrs. Piper. 30 of those people actually knew George Pellew before he died. Mrs. Piper, however had never met Pellew when he was living.

Pellew, speaking through Mrs. Piper, was able to identify 29 of the 30 people who happened to have known him before he died, none of whom were known to the medium. The only person Mr. Pellew could not properly identify was a childhood friend whom Pellew had not seen in decades. The 29 people he identified easily and correctly, were convinced by the mannerisms Pellew exhibited through the medium, Mrs. Piper, that they had in fact spoken with George Pellew, still living in the afterlife. Many were willing to testify that they had communicated with a disembodied, surviving consciousness who appeared to be George Pellew. This case is wonderfully told in Deborah Blum's 2006 book *Ghost Hunters*.

4. FREDRICK H.W. MYERS ADC[47] **– The Cross Correspondences:**[5] This is one of the most famous of all After-Death communications because it was lead posthumously from the other side by one of the great minds of psychical research Fredrick H.W. Myers. Widely known as the *Cross Correspondences* Myers' devised this double blind study which he actually conducted from the other side using ADC beginning six years after his own death. Myers sent scraps of messages back from the afterlife to five mediums on three continents. Scraps purposefully delivered in foreign languages not familiar to the mediums, these scraps would only make sense if collected and pieced together by the British Society for Psychical Research (B-SPR). Here is that story.

Myers, who was a founding member of the B-SPR in 1882, died 19 years later in 1901, and a few years after his death, Myers started sending messages back from the other side to these five mediums. He continued doing this for over 30 years following his death. Eventually, two other members of the B-SPR, former colleagues of Myers also died, and shortly thereafter they joined Myers in this project from the other side. The three of them actually joined up in the afterlife and continued their work for the B-SPR together from beyond the grave.

These deceased B-SPR members sent parts of each message to the different mediums like pieces of a puzzle. Quoting very obscure Greek and Latin poetry, which would be unknown to the mediums who did not know Greek or Latin. These mediums recorded these scraps through entranced (automatic) writing. Much of this writing made its way to the SPR in England where it was later pieced together.

> *To each automatist (a medium who does automatic writing) the information would be so fragmentary and strange as to be meaningless; but when pieced together, it could carry information of a kind that only could have come from Myers himself..."[48]*

> Brian Inglis

This double blind test carried out by Myers and his deceased SPR colleagues purposefully involved transmitting so disjointedly to provide a double blind communication in order to silence all the skeptics simply by showing that it could not have been one medium's idea, but that it was actually Myers' consciousness communicating back from the afterlife. He knew that if there was any way a skeptic could say that the mediums "imagined it" or that it was a hoax, or that they could read each other's minds, that they would attempt to do so.

Consequently, Myers set it up where no medium would know what the other was doing. What Myers and his colleagues did was no easy task, and quite difficult to orchestrate when they had to coordinate the activities of five mediums on three continents doing it all through the power of ESP from the other side. *You can google Cross Correspondences to read all about this.*

5. RUNKI'S ADC:[49] In Reykjavik, Iceland a séance circle lead by Hafsteinn Bjornsson had been meeting for seances in 1937 and 1938, but suddenly, in 1939, Runolfur Runolfsson, or Runki, a disembodied consciousness began to come through at each meeting.

Recently, a new member had joined the circle named Ludvik. When Ludvik began to attend, Runki, began speaking through the medium and revealed that, in October 1887 (52 years earlier), he had been out drinking with friends. On his way home that evening after the drinking party he was drunk and so lay down and fell asleep on the rocky seashore. Unfortunately, the tide came in and he was drowned and then swept out to sea. Runki said, "I was carried in by the tide, but the dogs and ravens tore me to pieces." Later the remnants of his body were buried in a nearby grave, but his thigh-bone was missing. The bone, according to Runki, was "carried out to sea again, to later wash up on the beach at Sandgerti, There it was passed around, and it is now in Ludvik's House".

However, Ludvik knew nothing of any bone. Later inquiries among the oldest people in the community of Sandgerti, turned up memories of a very tall man's leg bone, which had been found on the beach. Also, for reasons that no one could remember 52 years later, the bone was reported to have been placed in the interior wall of the house which was now occupied by Ludvik. Subsequently, a large leg bone was retrieved from the inside wall of Ludvik's house. It was then verified that Runki had indeed been a very tall man.

Of course, now the question comes up about why does the disembodied consciousness of Runki, still need his thigh bone fifty years later? But, the fact that this story illustrates is that Runki's consciousness was still continuing somewhere, half a century after his physical death.

> You can Google Runolfur Runolfsson, or Runki to find numerous references to this incident. Also, if you go to http://www3.hi.is/~erlendur/english/mediums /gudni.pdf and down load a PDF file of Erlendur Haraldsson and Ian Stevenson's report on Runki published in the Journal of the American Society for Psychical Research Vol. 69 July 1975

6. MONTAGUE KEEN ADC:[50] Montague (Monty) Keen, aged 79, one of Britain's more prominent researchers in psychic phenomena, died of a heart attack while speaking at the podium on January 15, 2004, during a public debate with a skeptic, at the Royal Society for the Arts in London. A few weeks later his wife Veronica, contacted University of Arizona Scientist Gary Swartz Ph.D, and reported that she had received messages from her deceased husband, through several different mediums, all stating that Monty wanted to conduct some research with Dr. Swartz, whom he had met several years earlier, prior to his own death. Dr. Swartz and his research associate Julie Beischel then designed a two part double blind research project involving several mediums. One of the mediums they used was Allison DuBois, whose career as a psychic legal investigator the NBC program "Medium" is based on. During the reading DuBois did not know anything about the subject of the reading, but Monty, speaking through DuBois, described his death as, "falling at the podium", and then Monty referred to an upcoming event which was dedicated to his memory, and which had been scheduled after his death. So, here we have the deceased speaking about events which were not on any calendar before he died and which are unknown to the medium. Further, he said, speaking through the medium, that this event was a, "somewhat flattering surprise". He also said through the medium, that their communication in this way would be an excellent "White Crow". Dr. Swartz then questioned the medium, who it is apparent from the transcript, had no idea what significance the reference to "White Crow" might have had. There were several additional facts conveyed through the medium which were unknown to both the medium and the sitters, but which were know to Monty, which prove that it was his disembodied consciousness speaking from the other side through the medium. This entire séance was video taped by the University of Arizona Research Laboratory.

Monty had been a member of the British Society of Psychical Research for over 55 years. I have read the published transcript of that DuBois reading. It is clear that Monte has just replicated the type of proof from the other side that Fredric H.W. Myers had provided in the famous Cross Correspondence work 100 years earlier. Monty communicated that:

"The thing about the after-life that stood out for him, and that made him so happy is how he could still be here so much after his passing, and, how he would feel energy-wise, like he did when he was younger instead of with the issues he had accumulated as he got older." [50]

Monte Keen, from the other side

The researchers concluded that the medium was definitely receiving information related to the designated deceased, which was outside the possibility of telepathy. And they further stated:

"These kinds of observations provide compelling evidence, if not convincing evidence, that intention, choice and intelligence, and hence some sort of personal consciousness, survive bodily death". [51]

Gary E. Swartz, PhD & Julie Beischel, PhD, Univ.of

Arizona 2005

His wife Veronica Keen, has also reported that Monty did fully materialize (apparition) at a séance with medium David Thompson in England about a month after Monty's death, and there have been other communications from him recorded in New Zealand, Ireland and the United States. He has reported that "His work is even more important", where he now is, "than the work he was doing in the physical".

DREAM COMMUNICATIONS:

THE BIBLE SPEAKS OF DREAM COMMUNICATIONS: In the Old Testament the Bible's speaks of Daniel interpreting dreams as did the old testament Joseph (Yura) interpret dreams for the Pharaoh when he was in Egypt. Jungian psychologists today provide the same service as Daniel in using the symbols of dream interpretation to study the sub-conscious mind. This is in fact very similar to using the symbols of the Tarot cards to interpret the desires of our hearts. Yet, both Jungian dream interpretation and Tarot are passive methods of observation or "mind reading" and only reveal our present perspective.

Further, in the New Testament Joseph, the husband of Mary the mother of Jesus, twice got messages through dreams. So it is clearly evident that the Bible endorses communications from spirits through dreams as being a valid medium.

So, when these "approved" scriptures present both clairvoyance and speaking to disincarnate spirits as biblical truths practiced by both the old testament people and also by the apostolic Christians. Why is it that the churches no longer allow this form of communications? Why aren't these same practices of spirit communications through mediums and dream visitations considered to be just as valid today for modern Jews, Christians and Muslims? Why do they discourage Tarot readings and dream interpretation? Could it be that these *religions of the book* will lose control when people no longer need their learned scholars to interpret God's will?

DREAM COMMUNICATION IS OPEN TO EVERYONE: Each of us is gifted with this psychic ability to dream, and our dream symbols can also be manipulated by a deceased consciousness to communicate with us. So, you might ask, "if dream communication is so simple, then why haven't your own dead relatives communicated with you?" The short answer is that you have not been making yourself accessible to them.

In the case of Helen Duncan mentioned earlier, the dead sailor's mother was in attendance at Mrs. Duncan's séance at the exact moment of his death and so he came through to her immediately. Also, in the case of Monte Keen his wife regularly attends séances and so he communicated with her almost immediately after dying. So, you might consider just when have you attended a séance in order to make yourself accessible to your departed loved ones? Or, have you ever requested your dead loved ones to speak to you in a dream?

When the living don't make themselves accessible it is more difficult for the departed consciousness of a loved one to communicate. For example, it took Chaffin four years to finally get through to his son through a dream about the missing will. For four years he had a very important message to get across, but, he had to learn how to do this from the other side.

A PERSONAL DREAM COMMUNICATION: Here is a personal account of my own experience with spirit communications through dreams. After my father's death I repeatedly asked my father to contact me in a dream. I methodically established p-car resonance by asking him day and night to communicate with me while I was working in Houston Texas in 2005, some 6 months after he died. After about two weeks of asking him repeatedly to contact me, he finally did so.

Now, normally I don't remember any dreams at all. Hardly once a year am I even able to recall a dream. But, I continued to small talk with my father's deceased spirit throughout the day and evening for more than two weeks. "I need you to contact me"………."I know we weren't close when you were alive, but if you see it differently now and want to truly do me a favor, then contact me in a dream"…."Daddy, I am placing a note pad here by the bed with a pen so you can contact me…..". that very first night that I placed a note pad by the bed, he came through in a dream as if I had made a specific appointment.

Frankly, the dream would have to be unmistakably from him, and who a dream message is from is usually indicated by that person appearing in the dream. Also, for me to record it, the dream would have to disturb me enough to wake me up completely so that I could write it down. In my whole life of the two or three dreams I have been able to record I have only recorded one dream that did not awaken me in a fright.

CHAPTER 5

AFTER DEATH COMMUNICATIONS

"We have no warrant for the assumption that the phantom seen, even though it be somehow caused by a deceased person, is that deceased person, in any ordinary sense of the word."[42]

Fredric W.H. Myers

"I confess that at times I have been tempted to believe that the Creator has eternally intended this department of nature to remain baffling, to prompt our curiosities and hopes and suspicions all in equal measure, so that, although ghosts and raps and messages from spirits are always seeming to exist they can never be fully explained away."

Dr. William James, 1905

HOW MANY PEOPLE REALLY BELIEVE IN AN AFTERLIFE? In the last chapter we looked at the statistics for reincarnation and found that one in four people believe in it. The statistics for belief in the afterlife show that more than half of all Americans believe in some form of consciousness survival. In 2007 AARP Magazine reported a survey which found that among the Americans interviewed:

"More than half of those responding reported a belief in spirits or ghosts – with more women (60 percent) and men (44 percent) agreeing they believed in ghosts. Boomers are more likely to believe in ghosts (64 percent) when compared with those in their 60's (51 percent) or 70's or older (38 percent). Their belief is not entirely based on hearsay evidence, either, Thirty-eight percent of all those responding to our poll say they have felt a presence or seen something, that they thought might have been a spirit or a ghost"[43]

Sep/Oct 2007 AARP Magazine

One of the strongest proofs of the afterlife accessible to the average person, is an After-Death communication (ADC). It provides your heart with a new form of personal gnosis about the continued existence of a loved one. This knowing is difficult for others, who haven't experienced it, to contradict. One way to prove that human consciousness survives bodily death would be to establish reliable communications with those in the afterlife. In the 1880's, two societies formed for this exact purpose. In Great Britain in 1882, the Society for Psychical Research (SPR) formed, and a sister organization the American Society for Psychical Research (A-SPR) formed in 1884. These two organizations attracted a membership of world class scientists and have collected data from hundreds of mediums communicating with disincarnate souls, and documented hundreds of apparitions of the recently dead.

COMMUNICATION THROUGH MEDIUMS:

When we speak of mediums, we are talking about the oldest and most powerful form of psychical power, which in the middle ages was called "witchcraft" by the materialist minded disbelievers, and is still thought to be "of the devil" by the fundamentalist Christians. But, what is actually taking place is not any form of witchcraft and has nothing to do with evil forces or imagined devils. The medium or "sensitive" is merely a person with a certain psychic gift which is often inherited and that allows them to establish what physicists today would call a p-car resonance (quantum coherence) with the specific consciousness which is the subject of the desired communication. In other words, "dial up their wavelength".

One of the earliest cases of After Death communication (ADC) with the deceased comes from the Bible's Old Testament in the book of Samuel. This specific case bears examination because of the conundrum it presents to Christian believers who, for doctrinal reasons, wish to discredit After-Death communications. This conundrum arises for Christians due to the following reasons:
- If every word in the Bible is literally true, as they want to claim it is, and
- If the Bible also clearly speaks of After-Death communications as being a reality, then
- Communications with the dead must, by their own standards of Biblical truth, be completely valid.

THE WITCH OF ENDOR: In 1 Samuel 28, verses 7-15, the story of the *Witch of Endor* is probably the oldest widely reported case of an

After Death communication (ADC) Here the medium calls forth the consciousness of a disincarnate soul to speak through the medium to those still living.

Here is the story:

> King Saul said, "Find me a woman who is a medium so I may go and inquire of her".
>
> "There is one in Endor", they said. So Saul disguised himself putting on other clothes and at night he and two men went to the woman.
>
> "Consult a spirit for me" he said, "and bring up for me the one I name"
>
> But, the woman said to him "Surely you know what Saul has done. He has cut off the mediums and spiritists from the land. Why have you set a trap for my life to bring about my death?"
>
> "Saul swore to her by the Lord, "As surely as the Lord lives, you will not be punished for this."
>
> Then the woman answered, "Who shall I bring up for you"
>
> "Bring up Samuel". He said.
>
> When the woman saw Samuel, she cried out at the top of her voice and said to Saul, "Why have you deceived me? You are Saul!"
>
> The King said to her, "Don't be afraid. What do you see".
>
> The woman said, "I see a spirit coming up out of the ground".
>
> "What does he look like", he asked.
>
> "An old man wearing a robe is coming up", she said.
>
> Then Saul knew it was Samuel, and he bowed down and prostrated himself with his face to the ground.
>
> Samuel said to Saul, "Why have you disturbed me by bringing me up?"
>
> 1 Samuel 28: 7-15 (NIV)

In 13 verses that follow, King Saul goes on to tell his troubles and the disincarnate Samuel predicts Saul's coming downfall and defeat. During his prior physical life Samuel had been a famous seer (clairvoyant), and in this biblical text Samuel's dis-embodied consciousness still retained this power of *second sight* (clairvoyance) even in the afterlife and predicts Saul's future. Not exactly in accord with main stream Christian doctrine, but in strict accordance with After-Death communications as understood by the Society for Psychical Research and Spiritualists throughout the world..

So, according to the literal words in the Bible, the following things are true:

- There is an afterlife, where our disincarnate consciousness goes on living.
- Mediums can communicate with the consciousness of dead persons by establishing p-car resonance (quantum coherence, see chapter 6)
- The so-called dead retain their psychic abilities in the afterlife (Samuel was seeing the future).

In this story the deceased Samuel, speaking from beyond the grave, predicted the outcome of Saul's upcoming battle. That action by Samuel indicates that the deceased consciousness was responding in real time by predicting a future event for mortals living here in time and space. Therefore, it is not the medium merely making a psychometric reading through p-car resonance of a recorded memory of Samuel which is stored in a holographic record, but instead the deceased consciousness of Samuel was practicing the same talent of clairvoyance from beyond the grave, which he had demonstrated when previously living a physical life. Consequently, if the Bible is true, and if then this story is true, then After-Death communications are also true.

Unfortunately, this whole idea of After-Death communications is so upsetting to many Christian believers that after realizing the Bible admits ADC is valid, instead of advancing to the higher level of thinking which honesty demands they may instead try desperately to hold on to their now obsolete but still comfortable beliefs. So, while admitting that mediums do actually communicate with the dead, as is stated in their Bible, they may ignorantly parrot the rote response taught them by the church by quickly saying that the medium doing the communication is, "of the devil".

This feeble response is left over from the ignorance of the dark ages, and is exactly the type of manipulation of the average citizen which emperor Justinian had in mind. This same medieval idea that it is, "of the devil", is how this medium in *1 Samuel* got nicknamed the *Witch* of Endor, even though the scriptural account nowhere refers to her as a witch. But, leaving the such sophomoric religious controversy behind let's look at some very interesting After-Death communications.

INTERESTING 20th Century AFTER DEATH COMMUNICATIONS:

Here are several modern cases which have been documented by ADC researchers, and which you can look up on line for yourself:

1. HMS BARNUM ADC:[44] During the Second World War, in 1944, an English medium Mrs. Helen Duncan, was conducting one of her regular séances for a group of women in Birmingham, England. During the session she was spontaneously interrupted by the disincarnate consciousness of a recently drowned man, who claimed to have been a sailor from the crew of HMS Barnum (a British warship), He contacted this séance and reported that his ship had just then been sunk by the Germans because he wanted to communicate this to his mother who was attending that séance. Speaking through the medium, Helen Duncan, he told his mother that everyone aboard including himself had drowned.

Unfortunately, British Naval Intelligence, who did not want this classified information about the ship's sinking to get out, arrested Mrs. Duncan and accused her of the crime of witchcraft under a law dating back over 200 years to 1735. Unfortunately, the Navy continued the prosecution and Mrs. Duncan was actually convicted of this ancient crime of *witchcraft*, and was sent to prison.

Now, it is apparent from the facts of the case that her only *crime* was that she knew and told the truth which was being related to her by the disincarnate spirit of the drowned sailor. British Prime Minister, Sir Winston Churchill was adamant at the time that Mrs. Duncan had not committed any crime and should be immediately released. However, being that it was wartime, British Naval Intelligence won the day and kept Mrs. Duncan in prison until the war was over the following year.

Winston Churchill was actually so moved by this travesty of justice that he then bothered to have all the anti-witch laws in Great Britain repealed so that today in the United Kingdom, witches have the same rights and freedoms as any clergy.

Finally, in 1998, 54 years later, according to a news story reported by Reuters, a full pardon was finally being processed for Mrs. Duncan. *To check this story online go to the HMS Barnum Association at www.hmsbarnum.com, click on THE SHIP, and then click on the HELEN DUNCAN STORY.*

The simple fact remains that either:
- Mrs. Duncan was actually communicating with a dead sailor and was receiving sensitive classified information from the other side in real time, or
- British Naval Intelligence is a foolish organization that believes in witches.

Frankly, I don't believe that British Naval Intelligence is that foolish. But, following is another example you can also check out on line.

2. CHAFFIN'S WILL ADC:[45] The 1927 proceedings of the SPR documents the case of a North Carolina Farmer named Chaffin. Chaffin had written a will in 1905 which left all his money and property to his third son, and disinherited his other two sons, and his wife.

But, Chaffin did not die until sometime after 1920 and that 1905 will was not his last will and testament. Unfortunately, after his death no later wills were found and that 1905 will was the only one available.

However, four years after his death, one of the disinherited sons, James, began to have a series of vivid visions of his father during a night of restless sleep. The apparition of his father kept telling him, "You will find my will in the overcoat pocket".

James, was moved by these vivid dreams and later located his father's overcoat in the possession of a third brother. Together, the two brothers carefully examined the coat and located a paper sewn into the lining. Ripping out the lining they found a note card, which said, "Read the twenty-seventh chapter of Genesis in my Daddy's old Bible".

Their mother still had that Bible, which was now so old that it fell apart when they opened it. But, it did contain a later holographic will dated 1919, which was clearly written in Chaffin's own hand writing and which divided the property equally between the three sons. The handwriting of the will was checked and found to be clearly that of Chaffin, and therefore this second "found will" was not contested in court, but was allowed to stand.

who remember past lives, and while final scientific replication must perhaps wait my heart still intuitively believes Dr. Weiss.

In any case, Dr. Weiss' experiences are great reading, he is eloquent, compelling and an honest guy who clearly says, **"The afterlife is very real"**. As quoted below from his excellent book *Messages from the Masters* ©2000:

> *"I believe we do reincarnate, until we learn our lessons and graduate", and I have repeatedly pointed out that there is much historical and clinical evidence that reincarnation is a reality."*
>
> Brian Weiss, M.D.

> *"I have become aware that an entire spiritual philosophy has been gently unfolded and handed to me......Our consciousness has finally evolved into accepting this filtered wisdom of the ages.....We are swimming in a sea of New Age, holistic, and spiritual awareness that seems to have flooded over the dams on old beliefs and constricted consciousness.....the evidence is everywhere that New Thought is becoming mainstream."*
>
> Brian Weiss, M.D

I was personally privileged to hear Brian Weiss speak in San Francisco in February 2002, and I spoke with him afterwards. During his presentation he mentioned several additional cases which had come to him recently, which I later researched and I believe you will find interesting:

JENNY COCKELL / MARY SUTTON:[36] This is a great read and Jenny's book is available from Amazon.com. Jenny, is an English housewife with two children, who like Dr. Ian Stevenson's subjects spontaneously remembered, beginning in early childhood, that she had lived a prior life in Ireland, where she had eight children, but she had died before those children were fully grown. From childhood on Jenny drew pictures of her house and a map of the shoreline and her church which had an unusual façade. She researched Irish maps looking for the town of *Malaheit*. After she found it she traveled there and felt that it was the place where she had lived before. She found both the church and her former home. The home had become a ruin and had been empty since the 1950's. But, she believed she had lived there in the 1920's or 30's, and that she had been named Marry Sutton. She also believed that she had died from the complications of child birth leaving behind her children. So, she kept inquiring.

Today, Jenny has managed to reunite with the five of Mary Sutton's eight children who are still living, and she has also found the room in a Dublin hospital where Mary (her former self) died. Four of the children (all older than Jenny), believe that she is their deceased mother Mary, because of all the things she can remember about their lives together. The fifth child prefers to believe that Mary speaks to Jenny from another dimension, telling details to Jenny. But, Jenny emphatically tells her formert child, "No, I am actually Mary".

JEFFERY J. KEENE / JOHN B. GORDON:[37] Another case which is also a great read is Jeffery Keene, who sells his book online (just google him). Mr. Keene, had a strange experience when he was drawn to a civil war battlefield. On that battle field he had visions and heard things including a particular phrase, "Not yet", the significance of which, at the time, he did not understand. He chronicles his investigations and discoveries, including the fact that he looks nearly exactly like, and also has scars on his face arms and legs similar to the wounds received by a specific Civil War soldier, John B. Gordon. That soldier survived the battle and was later a statesman in Virginia and there are several surviving photographs of Gordon. Jeffery Keene compares those photos with his own photos and his resemblance to Gordon is uncanny. They really look like the very same guy.

CAPT. BOB SNOW: This gentleman is a homicide detective in Indianapolis, Indiana, He participated in regression therapy, and got twenty eight clues from a remembered past life. The clues were recorded on tape. He spent the next couple of years investigating those clues and discovered that he was an artist named James Carol Beckwith who died in 1917. He describes how he did the detective work on those clues in an episode on the Sci-Fi channel which is available online as a video at http://vodpod.com/watch/1310417-reincarnation-proof

CHILDREN OF THE HOLOCAUST:
Dr. Weiss also spoke of a Swedish psychologist who has worked with over 200 young people who remember prior lives in the German concentration camps or World War II. That psychologist has gone back to Poland and other locations of the concentration camps and

has validated the accuracy of over two dozen of these children's memories.

For example, *some of these people who are now 30 years old read their concentration camp numbers as if they were tattooed on their arms.* Later, when the prior identity associated with that ID number is found in the camp records, it is found that these 30 year olds are remembering the proper details of the lives of those concentration camp victims who had that same I.D. number, but who are now dead.

1974 - Teuvo Koivisto born into a Lutheran Christian family in Helsinki, Finland August 20, 1971. At the age of 3 years old, he told his mother that he had been alive before. Teuvo explained that he was told that he was being taken to the "bathroom," but he was taken instead to this big "furnace" room. People were then told to undress and their gold teeth and eyeglasses were taken from them. People were then put in the "furnace" room. He told how gas came out of the walls and he could no longer breathe. *Check it out at, www.iisis.net/...jewish-concentration-camp...change-religion&hl=en_US*

1957 - Barbro Karlen was born to Christian parents in Sweden in 1954. When she was less than three years old, Barbro told her parents that her name was not Barbro, but Anne Frank. This was less than ten years after Anne Frank had died in the Bergen-Belsen concentration camp in 1945. Barbro's parents had no knowledge of who Anne Frank might have been. The book, <u>Anne Frank: Diary of a Young Girl</u>, also known as <u>The Diary of Anne Frank</u>, had not yet been translated or published in Swedish.

Barbro states how her parents desired that she call them "Ma" and "Pa," but because she knew that they were not her real parents. Barbro instead said that her real parents would soon come to get her and take her away to her real home. While still a child Barbro told her parents details of her life as Anne. Barbro also had nightmares as a child, in which men ran up the stairs and kicked in the door to her family's attic hiding place, all of this with no knowledge of the story of Anne Frank. *Check it out at, www.iisis.net/...frank-barbro-karlen-reincarnation-past-life&hl=en_US*

JEWISH BELIEFS ABOUT REINCARNATION: Rabbi Yonassan Gershom, a Hasidic storyteller, teacher, and writer, has published several essays on Jewish spirituality that have appeared in numerous periodicals and anthologies. He has published three books on the subject:

- *Jewish Tales of Reincarnation,*[38] a collection of 70 traditional and modern stories about Jewish reincarnation.
- *Beyond the Ashes,*[39] is his account of personal encounters with hundreds of people from all walks of life, who have shared their memories of visions, dreams, and flashbacks that seem to becoming from another life during the Nazi Holocaust. He also presents Jewish teachings about karmic cycles, the levels of the soul, views of the afterlife and reincarnation in Judaism, as seen in the light of traditional Jewish texts and modern discoveries. and
- *From Ashes to Healing.*[40] completes the saga begun in the first book by presenting fifteen testimonies of people who have past-life memories, visions, and dreams about the Holocaust.

This all dovetails with many of Stevenson's reincarnation cases investigated in Southeast Asia where the children specifically remember being Japanese Soldiers in their prior lives.

ARAMAIC TWINS: Another anecdote Dr. Weiss described in my personal notes from his lecture is that a set of 3 year old twins, who spoke their own language to each other. I later found a reference on his recommended reading list for the following book which tells the story:

In the book *Reincarnation: The Phoenix Fire Mystery,* compiled by Joseph Head and S.L. Cranston describes the case of twin baby boys who were born in the United States but who spoke with each other in a strange, unrecognizable language. At Columbia University's language department a professor of ancient languages identified that the babies were speaking Aramaic, a language which has not been in use since the time of Christ. The babies' father was Dr. Marshall McDuffie, a prominent New York physician, and his wife Wilhelmina.

OTHER LIVES OTHER SELVES: Another educated scientist who is speaking out is an Oxford trained Jungian psychologist, Roger J. Woolger, PhD, currently living in Burlington, Vermont, who believes fully in reincarnation through his own experiences with past life regression therapy. His seminal book *Other Lives, Other Selves,*[41] published in 1988, has a marvelous first chapter chronicling his own conversion from skeptic to believer. His book goes on to differentiate between individual past lives and a more Jungian view of

karmic collective consciousness or **"shared" past lives**, which casts
past life memories in a very different light, and could explain how
multiple people alive today could remember the same past life.
Maybe, all seven people who remember being Napoleon actually
were previously Napoleon, or maybe Napoleon had a split personality and each of them is just one of those. The endless possibilities
boggle the mind, yet, it is obvious that we know something about
reincarnation, but not all.

PETER PANDOER - RASA YOGA: I am not a follower of
Yoga, but I appreciate the excellent explanation of reincarnation
which Peter Pandoer gives including his discussion of memories of
past lives, the Near-Death experience etc. This is contained on 14
segments (each about 5 minutes long) created by Peter speaking on
dharma and reincarnation. He explains reincarnation speaking
from a Hindu/yoga religious perspective in a video summary which
parallels mine on all this. It is online at www.youtube.com/user/
peterpandoer/videos Careful there are 155 videos on his site and
you are looking for the REINCARNATION SERIES 1-14.

Go to the website and scroll down and pick Page 2, where you will
find most of the 14 segments which are not in order and some of
which appear on page 3. Be careful to click on REINCARNATION
and not on the similar 15 part series on THE TRUTH which are
mixed in on the site and have the same title picture, But, start with
REINCARNATION segment 1 and go through the 14 (note 10 is a
repeat of 9). If you don't have time for all of them then listen to
only Reincarnation 6 and 7. But, truly all 14 are worth the effort in
order to understand yoga's viewpoint. Pandoer will be explaining it
in the context of yoga, If you are not into Yoga practice you can start
with session 2, but in any case you will need to know several definitions:

- **Dharma** is the path here in this life of righteousness and living one's
  life according to the codes of conduct as described by the Hindu scrip-
  tures.
- **Jiva** = soul / consciousness.
- **Prana** = vital life.
- **Pranic body** = physical body.
- **Praeta** = Ghost
- **Samadi**, a higher level of concentrated meditation (i.e. crossing over to
  the other side).
- **Samsara** = the cycle of birth, life, death, rebirth or reincarnation, con-
  notation is often "life here on earth"
- **Samskara** = is a rite of passage.

If you listen to this whole series Pandoer wisely explains much about Hebrew beliefs, Jesus' beliefs, and even Constantine I as well as Near-Death and Reincarnation, all things which took me 40 years to carefully research, but which you can hear him explain in an hours listening.

CONCLUSION:

You can look deeper into the referenced literature in the end notes and find additional evidence for reincarnation. On the other hand, to date I have personally found no evidence at all for the opposing view that reincarnation is not valid. Near Death survivors have not been returning saying, "There is nothing over there", and no one to date has reported remembering a prior non-existence. So, not only the preponderance of evidence, but all the evidence is entirely on the side of reincarnation. The fact is there are actually hundreds of rigorously documented White Ravens.

come to believe that James Linegar is actually her brother reincarnated. She believes this simply because of all the things little James knows that only her deceased brother could have known. His parents published their story *Soul Survivor* in 2010 as end noted above. There are five videos available on the net which tell his story, four are episodes from the TV show *Prime Time: The Unexplained*, narrated by Charles Gibson, They can all be watched at the following URL's

- http://www.victorzammit.com/evidence/childrenwhor ememberpastlives.htm

- http://www.youtube.com/watch?v=5965wcH2Kx0&feat ure=related
- http://vodpod.com/watch/6558256-reincarnation-proof-of-true-story-caught-on-camera-that-shocks-the-world-

6. CASE OF CORLISS CHOTKIN, JR.[33] It is a common belief of the Tlingit Indians in South Eastern Alaska and Western British Columbia that dead persons return to this world to live again, but only do so among their relatives. If the pregnant mother has a dream and remembers a dead person, or the child when born has a birthmark similar to a deceased relative, they name the child after the deceased relative. Dr. Stevenson reports several Tlingit cases in his book Twenty Cases Suggestive of Reincarnation. Here is the story of Corliss Chotkin, Jr.

Victor Vincent, a full blooded Tlingit, died in the spring of 1946. For the last years of his life Victor had felt very close to his niece, Mrs. Corliss Chotkin, Sr. the daughter of his sister. Sometime in the Spring of 1945, about a year before his death, while visiting this niece, Victor said to her,

"I'm coming back as your next son. I hope I don't stutter as much as I do now, and your son will have these scars".

He then pulled up his shirt and showed her the scar on his back where he had had surgery. He also pointed to the scar on his nose on the right side at the base.

On December 15, 1947, 18 months after the death of Vincent, Mrs. Corliss Chotkin gave birth to a son. At birth the boy had two scars exactly where predicted, which matched Vincent's scars. When his mother was teaching the child to say his name, he said, *"Don't you know me, I'm Kahkody,"* which had been Vincent's tribal name. When he was two the child was being wheeled along the street in a stroller when he spontaneously recognized a step daughter of Victor and called her correctly by name saying *"There's my Susie"*. He was the first to have recognized her. He hugged her and also spoke her Tlingit name. No one had introduced them nor told him her name. Also when he was two he recognized Vincent's son William, He spontaneously spotted William on the street and said *"There's William my son"*. At a large public meeting he picked out Vincent's widow in the crowd and announced *"There's my old lady"* identifying her also as Rose, which was her correct name. He also spontaneously recognized four other people former fiends of Vincent, on occasions when the family recorded the fact, all occurring before he turned six years old. Corliss also narrated two stories about the life of Vincent, which his mother believes no one could have told him. He also easily repaired engines with no lessons, Vincent was also a natural mechanic.

There are hundreds of cases similar to these which Ian Stevenson has documented and published accounts of and I encourage you to study them in the available literature.

7. CHIEF CUMSHEWA:[34,35] My own personal experience of this unquestioned belief in reincarnation among the Pacific Northwest Indians comes from a voyage I made in 1994 to the ruins of the village Koona (Skedans) in the Queen Charlotte Islands in Western British Columbia. These islands are 60 miles out in the Pacific ocean west of Prince Rupert, B.C. and don't always appear on BC highway maps. The Haida culture there, like the Tlingit culture on the mainland (especially in the village of Koona (Skedans) which historically was very social with Tlingit villages on the mainland), teaches that the spirits of the deceased return in the following generations.

Chief Cumshewa (Charles Wesley) an elder of the Haida tribe in his 80's, whom I met there at Koona where he was serving as the Haida watchman/guide volunteered a story about a specific reincarnation, although I had never mentioned to him that I had any such interests. This came out while the chief was talking about his departed mentor Jim Jones. Mr. Wesley (Chief Cumshewa) said "My son Patrick is a Haida artist, and I believe that the spirit of Jim Jones lives in Patrick, who was born just after Jim died." I spoke with Mr. Wesley further on this and he told of how Patrick had the same traits as his deceased friend Jim. It was apparent to me from the way Mr. Wesley included these thoughts in everyday conversation that he found it quite normal to believe in reincarnation. Here is an excerpt from a magazine article I later published entitled *KOONA: Through the eyes of a Haida Chief*:

> *"To be guided through a ghost village, by a Haida elder with the venerable rank of a senior village chief, was an honor not lost on us. Cumshewa handed each of us a book entitled* Those Born at Koona, *"We'll start on page 14, when we get to the west end of the village", he said softly. We listened attentively, following as he lead us over Koona's sacred grounds, describing the village history in friendly but solemn terms. This was a great man, who was bringing the gift of age and experience to the sharing of his story: the story of both his people and his lifetime.*

> *"The chief, born three decades after Koona was abandoned in 1889, explained that his authority for knowledge of the village came from Jim Jones, whom Cumshewa had fished with, after the second world war. Jim had been born in Koona, and lived there until his teenage years. The Chief showed us Jim's photo in the back of the book, taken at Koona in 1954 when Jim was an old man. The Haida culture teaches that spirits of the deceased return in the following generations. And Cumshewa shared with us that, "My son Patrick, is a Haida artist, and the Spirit of Jim lives in Patrick, who was born just after Jim died".*

> *I spoke with Mr. Wesley (Chief Cumshewa) further on this and he told of how Patrick had the same traits as his deceased friend Jim. It was apparent to me from the way Mr. Wesley included these thoughts in everyday conversation that he found it quite normal to believe in reincarnation. Here was a wizened man whom I respected greatly, who believed that our consciousness returns for multiple lifetimes.*

PAST LIFE REGRESSIONS investigated by Dr. Brian Weiss:

Another field of research into past lives is the field of psychology known as *Past Life Regression Therapy*. Honestly, this is a fringe area of psychology, consequently, most of my Psychiatrist friends schooled in the Freudian tradition are wary of anyone practicing in this field, and my Jungian Psychologist friends are a little more welcoming, but also wary.

One prominent Psychiatrist who is a nationally recognized expert in this controversial area of Past Life Regression therapy is Dr. Brian Weiss, M.D. a practicing Psychiatrist and formerly Chief of Psychiatry at the hospital affiliated with the University of Miami. Dr. Weiss is convinced that reincarnation is real. He describes the problem this way,

> *"I have encountered some extremely talented people—psychics, mediums, healers and others—and I have encountered even more who have limited talent or skill and are mostly opportunists. But, I have also been careful not to throw out the baby with the bathwater. One person or one experience might be disappointing, but the next might be truly extraordinary and should not be discounted because of previous events".*

DR. WEISS' PROFESSIONAL BACKGROUND: Brian Weiss, M.D. was a disciplined, conservative scientist and physician who distrusted anything that could not be proved by the traditional scientific method. Graduating Phi Beta Kappa, magna Cum Laude at Columbia University in 1966, he received his M.D. at Yale University in 1970. Following internship at New York University-Bellevue Medical Center he completed residency in psychiatry at Yale. Next he taught at University of Pittsburg and University of Miami where he lead the pharmaceutical division. He became Associate Professor of Psychiatry at the U of M medical school, and Chief of Psychiatry at the University affiliated hospital, by which time he had already published 37 scientific papers and book chapters in his specialty field. Weiss is definitely not the type of recognized professional who would lightly espouse fringe ideas.

DR. WEISS' STORY: But in 1980, he met a new patient named Catherine. For 18 months Dr. Weiss used conventional methods of therapy attempting to overcome Catherine's symptoms, but when nothing else worked he tried using hypnosis. It was during a series of trance states that Catherine began to continually recall her "past-life" memories. Past lives that it was apparent she could not remember at all in her waking state.

In hypnotic trance Catherine also spoke of the time between lives. It was during one of these sessions while Catherine was in a trance state that Dr. Weiss was contacted by beings other than Catherine, who called themselves, "Masters". These were separate beings on the other side, who were in charge of Catherine's "curriculum". Also, to show Dr. Weiss that they were separate from Catherine these "Masters" told Dr. Weiss private things about himself that Catherine could not have known. One of these Masters told Dr. Weiss that he (the Master) had been incarnate in the flesh 86 different times. Catherine, while in a trance state, could recall some of what had taken place in her past lives, but *even in trance she could not recall any of the things these "Masters" had said* to Dr. Weiss through her.

Finally, Dr. Weiss decided after considerable contemplation, that regardless of any consequence that he might face as a professional M.D., such consequences would not prove to be as devastating as the personal consequences of not sharing the knowledge he had gained about immortality and the meaning of life. So, in spite of any damage to his own standing in the medical community he decided to go public with what he had learned.

In his books *Many Lives, Many Masters, Messages from the Masters,* and *Same Soul Many Bodies,* he tells his story in great detail and I recommend reading these books.

Basically, Weiss' books tell the same story as Dr. Ian Stevenson's books on reincarnation. Using regressive hypnotic therapy merely bypasses our forgetfulness and allows those of us who can't consciously remember our prior lives to access the information which is dormant in our subconscious. After reading Dr. Weiss' books it becomes easy to see that having past lives is quite *normal.*

Here are some of the specific things about reincarnation that these "Masters" told Dr. Weiss, (*italics are my inclusions*):

1. We chose when we will come into our physical state. (*This agrees with the Near Death experience of choosing to come back*).

2. We choose when we will leave, because we know when we have accomplished what we came here to do (*This agrees with the Near-Death experience, with the clarification that in the NDE such decisions are made on the other side of the veil*).

3. Everyone's path is the same. We must all learn Charity, Hope and Faith, and learn them well. The religious orders of all faiths have come closer to this than the others, because they have given up so much without being asked. The rest of us are always looking for rewards and justifications for our good behavior, but the reward is in the doing and not the getting. (*To understand a Christian mystic's view of this fact see the prayer of Saint Francis, or read Pierre Teilhard de Chardin*)

4. Patience is a virtue, everything comes with timing. Your life cannot be rushed, we must accept what comes to us at any given time, and not ask for more. We were never really born, we just pass through different phases and there is no end. There are many dimensions, but time is not as we see it (Consciousness is non-local and non-temporal). Progress is measured in lessons that are learned.

5. To be in the physical state is actually an *abnormal* condition. When you are in the spiritual state that is *normal* to you. The spiritual state (on the other side) is a state of renewal (R & R) it is a dimension like other dimensions. *This agrees with the Near-Death Experience......home is on the other side, with the light, while being here in reality is the less desirable state.*

6. You can waste much energy in fear. You must stop wasting energy in fear by instead releasing all fear and moving forward in love.

7. **If people knew that life is endless, that we will never die, and that we were never really born, then all fears would end.**

8. Apparently, we cannot learn as spirits because all learning requires feelings, and feelings are inherent in the flesh, where as spirits we do not "feel". *This agrees with the NDE.*

9. When we arrive on the other side we are usually burned out. We must go through a period of renewal, a period of contemplation and a period of decision to return to the flesh again. Our physical bodies are just a vehicle for us while we are in the flesh.

10. There are seven planes of existence each one consisting of many levels and we must pass through all seven before we return to the flesh. *This closely agrees with the ancient Egyptian religion of Thoth-Hermes, and parallels what Spiritualists have ascertained through After-Death communications (see chapter 5)*

11. Karma: We have debts that must be paid.......If we have not paid out these debts, then we must take them into another life.....in order that they can be worked through. You progress by paying your debts ("forgive us our debts as we forgive our debtors"). *Karma aggress with Plato, Buddhists, Origen, Jerome & St. Gregory.*

12. When we are in the flesh we will each have a dominant trait, lust, greed, etc. and you must learn to overcome that dominant trait, if not when you return again you will still carry that trait. With each life you go through when you do not fulfill these debts, the next life will be harder and more complicated, yet if you fulfill them you will find your next life to be easier. You choose it you are responsible for the life you have, it is your karma.

13. Wisdom is achieved very slowly. This is because intellectual knowledge is so easily acquired, but is not enough in itself. It must be transformed into 'emotional' or subconscious knowledge. Once it is so transformed then the imprint is permanent. Theoretical knowledge without practical application is simply not enough for your spirit's evolution.

14. Understand that no one is greater than any other.

A NOTE OF CAUTION: It is important to remember that, although this excellent philosophy agrees loosely with the NDE and the religion of the ancients, the jury is still out regarding the above stated ontology of the Masters until additional replication in double blind conditions can be acquired. To date, although several additional psychiatrists have also published similar findings of past life memories in patients through hypno-regression, none have yet reported similar discussions with these "Masters". On the other hand, the above stated world view does coincide well with the findings of Near-Death, After Death Communications and the children

But, when Marta was two and a half she began to speak, exactly as predicted by Sinha of. "When she had been big before". She volunteered to her parents that she had been neck-named Sinha in her prior life, and also that her real name in that prior live had been Maria.

Marta said all this despite the fact that the names Sinha and Maria had never once been uttered in their household. Marta made no less than 120 separate declarations over the next few years about details of Sinha's life. All were carefully recorded by her parents. Although, her former home from the first life was only 12 miles away, her father, in order to keep the single blind conditions, never took her there until she was 12 years old, although she had asked numerous times to go to her former home. And, it was not until the time of this visit at age 12 that the parents from the prior life heard anything about Marta being the reborn Sinha.

Dr. Ian Stevenson who has interviewed all the participants, except for the original deceased Sinha, has continued contact with Marta for many years, and in the 1974 edition of the book he describes Marta at age 54 after his most recent visit with her in Puerto Alegre in 1972.

"She is very much Marta, but still remembers much detail from her former life as Sinha, especially her bout with tuberculosis, and her death. She sees her prior life and this life as different chapters in a continuum".

When Marta was a child of three or four, and bereaved adults would suffer from grief, Marta would comfort them by saying,

"I died, and I am living again"

And another time, during a rainstorm, when one of her sisters expressed regret that their dead sister Emilia would get wet in the grave, the child Marta said,

"Don't say that, Emilia is not in the cemetery. She is in a safer and better place than we are; her soul never can be wet".

So, although Marta's memories have faded since the vivid days of her childhood. It is apparent from what she said in early childhood, that:

"As a child she also remembered her ten months of life on the other side between the two lives here."

47

I highly recommend reading this particular case in Dr. Stevenson's original report, in the book end-noted at the start of this section about Marta. The narrative runs 20 pages and is heavily documented and researched. Stevenson has interviewed all the significant participants, and the interesting story reads like a drama…….. And, so it seems that yet again we have another White Raven.

REVIVAL OF REINCARNATION AS A CHRISTIAN BELIEF:

Recently, a growing number of Christian theologians want to reconsider the discarded doctrine of reincarnation. Many realize that the butchered pieces of the Christian religion which remained after the Roman emperors had finished revising it to suit their desires, were not only incomplete, but were also not fully reclaimed during the Protestant reformation. Luther, Calvin, Wycliff, Hus, Tyndale, Zwingly and a host of others were all trying to relocate the original religion, but they were working against over 1000 years of the emperors obscuring the truth.

Geddes MacGregor, in his 1978 book[29] argues that reincarnation is fully compatible with Christianity and he makes five points. Why this is a compatible doctrine (*Italics are my inclusions*)
- There is strong scriptural evidence that Jesus taught reincarnation.
- The Christian scholars (Clement & Origen) at Alexandria wrote extensively about it in the second and third centuries, in the earliest written systematic theology in the Christian church's history.
- The church did not move against the belief in reincarnation for over 550 years, and even then did not condemn reincarnation, but, entirely at emperor Justinian's behest, merely shunned it.
- The doctrine is philosophically compelling because it satisfies our deepest instinct for justice, through Karma carried into future lives.
- Finally, MacGregor states that belief in reincarnation and karma offers the best explanation for a world in which there is much undeserved suffering and misfortune."

A DOCTRINE OF FAIRNESS: Reincarnation takes care of the problem of moral injustice. To the age-old question of Job (Why do the wicked prosper and the righteous suffer?) reincarnation has the simple answer:

"We are seeing in this life only a fragment of a long story.....Death is only the end of a chapter but not the end of the story."

Today, when empirical science has repeatedly documented the White Raven of reincarnation, and since there also is no church prohibition to believing in its reality but only the politically motivated decision "not to associate" with those who believe in reincarnation at emperor Justinian's behest, and when reincarnation is also found to be a doctrine believed by the early Christian fathers and also present in the "approved" scriptures,......... well maybe, it is time for authentic Christians to demand that their governing church bodies revive this early Christian belief, and officially recognize it to be the *normal* Christian doctrine that it originally was, as believed by the Jesus, Paul, the apostles and the majority of Christians for several hundred years after Christ and before the Roman emperors began revising the doctrines of the church.

Christian leaders of every denomination owe it to their Lord, and their faith, and their followers to carefully and completely study *all* the true facts, not accepting blindly what their church hierarchy may have been ignorantly parroting for the 1500 years since Justinian. When they have actually studied all the facts, and find the case for the single life theory to be lacking of any substance in the early church, they should then ask their churches governing bodies to revise their statements of faith to agree with Jesus instead of Justinian.

But, while we contemplate the Christian-ness of that doctrine, here are a few more White Ravens which are also heavily documented.

MORE CHILDREN'S MEMORIES FROM DR. STEVENSON

3. THE SHANTI DEVI CASE:[30] Shanti Devi was born in 1926 in old Delhi. At about the age of three she began to tell her parents stories regarding a former life, in which she was married to a man named Kedar Nath, who lived in the nearby town of Muttra. In that prior life she also had two children, and she had apparently died in child birth bearing a third child in 1925. She described in detail her home in Muttra where she had lived with her husband and children.

When her parents tired of trying to stop her from telling these stories, her grand uncle, Kishen Chand sent a letter to Muttra to see how much, if any, of the little girl's story was true. He mailed it to an address that Shanti herself remembered and gave to him. That same letter was received by a widower named Kedar Nath. His wife Lugdi had died in childbirth in 1925, the year before Shanti was born. Quite naturally, Kedar Nath suspected this was all a fraud. So he sent Mr Lal, his cousin, who lived in Delhi to visit Shanti at her home in Delhi. The cousin would know if she were an imposter.

Mr. Lal went to Shanti's home without announcing his relationship and pretending to be on business. But, when Shanti answered the door, she screamed and jumped into his arms. Her mother then came to the door, but before Lal could speak the nine year old Shanti said,

> *"Mother this is a cousin of my Husband! He lived not far from us in Muttra and then moved to Delhi. I am so happy to see him. He must come in, I want to know about my Husband and my sons."*

Mr. Lal confirmed for Shanti's parents all the facts she had told them over the years. Soon they reached the consensus that Kedar and his son should come to Delhi to meet Shanti. Later, when Kedar arrived Shanti, although only nine years old, treated him as a normal adult wife would do. She kissed him and called him by pet names. Shanti served him biscuits and tea. And then when Kedar's eyes began to fill with tears, she comforted him using personal phrases and pet names known only to Kedar and his former wife Lugdi Nath.

News reporters decided to sponsor Shanti on a trip to Muttra. They thought that she should be able to lead them to her former home. But, as the train arrived in Muttra, Shanti saw her former relatives from her prior life on the platform (relatives who had not been to Dehli, and whom she had not seen in this life). She yelled and waved at them as the train slowed at the platform. Before getting to meet the relatives she told the reporters that they were the mother and brother of her husband. On the platform she began to speak with them and the reporters noted that she had correctly named them. Then, **the reporters realized that nine year old Shanti was not speaking Hindustani, the language she spoke at home in Delhi, but was instead speaking coherently in a dialect specific to Muttra.** Shanti had never learned nor been exposed to this strange dialect, but according to the news reporters she already spoke it fluently, and if she actually was the deceased Lugdi's reincarnated consciousness, then she would easily know this local language.

Note: *this use of the dialect was reported in the news accounts, but could not later be verified by any eye-witnesses for Ian Stevenson during his research some decades later.*

Next, as the reporters had requested, Shanti lead them to the Nath house. Although, she had never been in Muttra during her current life she lead them directly to the Nath house. On the way she told them things that only Lugdi could have known . Her former husband Kedar asked her specifically where she had hidden some rings that Lugdi had owned before she died. Shanti told him that they were hidden in a pot which she had buried during her prior life in a location at their prior home where they had lived together before moving to this house. Later, the investigators were able to dig up the rings where she had said they were buried. The records also indicate that everyone who had previously known Lugdi in Muttra now accepted Shanti as being Lugdi's reincarnated consciousness.

Shanti's case has been investigated by numerous researchers over the years. Clearly, cases like this, with remembered foreign language, remembered buried objects, and spontaneously recognized faces from the prior life, are indeed rare. Yet, many of them do exist. And, just one such case, with so many facts revealed which were unknowable to anyone except the departed consciousness from the prior life, would seem to be all that is required as compelling prove that reincarnation actually happens. Again we have a third White Raven.

4. THE BONGKUCH PROMSIN CASE:[31] Bongkuch was born Februray 12, 1962 in the village of Don Kha in the Nakhon Sawan Province of Thailand. As soon as the child began to speak coherently, he started to repeatedly describe his prior life.

He said that he came form the village of Hua Tanon, which was nine kilometers away, and that his name in a prior life there had been Chamrat. He also gave his former parent's names. By the time he was two years old, he told details of his prior family and also that two men had murdered him at a fair in Hua Tanon, stabbing him in several places. He said they had taken his wristwatch and neck chain, and dragged his body into an open field. Bongkuch, also said that after his death as Chamrat, he stayed on a tree near the site of the murder for approximately seven years.

Then, one rainy day, he saw his present father passing by and decided to accompany him home on a bus. Bonkuch's father later recalled that he had attended a meeting in Hua Tanon not long before his wife became pregnant with Bongkuch. He also recalled that it had been raining. Bongkuch's parents had never heard of Chamrat's murder, except from Bongkuch.

Eventually, however, Chamrat's parents and friends heard about what Bongkuch had been saying, and some of them came to visit him in Don Kha, when he was two and a half years old. Through these contacts his parents eventually verified everything the young boy was saying about his prior life and the murder, which had taken place some ten years before.

Dr. Ian Stevenson later interviewed some of the policemen who investigated the original Murder, and they verified that the suspects in the case, one of whom fled, and the other who was aquitted for lack of evidence, were the same two people that Bongkuch had named as being his murderers.

Reports of Bonkuch's case appeared in the newspapers in Thailand in March 1965, and the director of the Government Hospital in Nakhon Sawan, a Dr. Sophon Nakphairaj sent copies of those reports to Ian Stevenson. Who began studying the case in 1966, and actually met Bongkuch in March 1980.

Bongkuch, often spoke Laotian words (Chamrat was Laotian) which his Thai parents did not understand. He also felt himself to be an adult, imprisoned in a child's body. He often made advances toward teenage girls, but would ignore girls his own age. Once, at a very young age, he attempted to fondle a teenage girl who was visiting his parents. Yet, by the time he was 18, he had nearly completely "moved on" from those childhood memories. Apparently this is another White Raven.

REINCARNATION IN NORTH AMERICA:

5. JAMES LINEGAR:[32] a 2 year old in Lafyette, Louisana remembered his prior life and being shot down during World War II on March 3, 1945 while flying his Navy Corsair over Chi Chi Jima as James Houston, a pilot flying from the Aircraft carrier *USS Natoma Bay CVE-62*, and remembered his friend Jack Larson a fellow pilot on the ship. His fellow pilot Jack Larson is still living. The child knew that his plane was hit near the engine and crashed in flames. Eye witnesses of his crash have verified the fact that his plane was hit in the engine. James Houston's sister is still living, and has now

SCIENCE AND REINCARNATION: On the other hand, there is now much rigorous Western science that fully supports reincarnation. At the University of Virginia in Charlottesville, the late Ian Stevenson, M.D. (1918 - 2007), former Carlson Professor of Psychiatry, studied this business of, "Taking life up again", for over 50 years from the early 1960's until well into this first decade of the 21st century.

Dr. Stevenson's colleagues (Bruce Greyson M.D., Jim Tucker, M.D., et al) are continuing his work which has to date cataloged and documented over 3000 individual cases of children who remember their past lives. This is all carefully documented using rigorous science to weigh the evidence in Stevenson's books; *Twenty Cases Suggestive of Re-incarnation*,[21] and *Children Who Remember Previous Lives*[22], Jim B. Tucker M.D. has also published on this same subject in 2005 in his book *Life Before Life* [23]

Stevenson has meticulously investigated thousands of cases in which children between three and five years old, begin relating memories of an earlier life to their new parents in the present life These children often have detailed accounts of their wives, husbands, and children from the previous life.

Often the children have graphic memories of how they died and/or who killed them. They can even recognize former friends and family members still living when they return to the vicinity where the previous life took place. In a few cases they can also remember the dialect of the prior home. In other cases they even carry a physical birthmark or physical deformity that corresponds with an injury received in the previous life. Stevenson published another book *Where Reincarnation and Biology Intersect*, which show photographically these corresponding deformities which match the prior incarnation.

Yet, by the time these children reach age 8-10 they usually begin forgetting the prior physical life as they assimilate into their current physical life. If they are surrounded by a culture which encourages these types of prior life memories then the memories may continue well into adulthood.

Unfortunately, in Western culture these cases often go unnoticed. When a child says, "I remember a past life", their parents, immersed in the Western cultural perspective of the *Single Life*

Theory, have traditionally shut them up if they spoke "such non-sense". Instead of listening to what the child might want to say American and European parents respond with, "Nonsense", or, "Mommy doesn't want to hear you say that again", and may even threaten punishment. But, in other cultures, where reincarnation is thought of as *normal,* these children are more likely to be listened to instead of being ostracized and told to, "shut up".

Yet, there has always been an undercurrent in Western culture and literature which acknowledges these memories. Consider the 18th century British Poet William Wordsworth.

> *"Our birth is but a sleep and a forgetting:*
> *The Soul that rises with us, our life's Star,*
> *Hath had elsewhere its setting,*
> *And cometh from afar:*
> *Not in entire forgetfulness,*
> *And not in utter nakedness,*
> *But trailing clouds of glory do we come*
> *From God, who is our home:"*

Ode to Intimations of Immortality
From RECOLLECTIONS OF Early Childhood
By, William Wordsworth (1770-1850)

SO, WHY DON'T ADULTS REMEMBER THESE PRIOR LIVES?

O.K., if there are children from the age of 3-5 who remember past lives then why don't you and I as adults remember our past lives?.......... Aren't these children simply imagining all this in their fairy tale world?... If these past life memories are real then shouldn't most adults remember them also?

Yet, most adults I have interviewed have almost no memories even from this present life of when they were three to five years old. So really, if they can't remember what they were doing in this current life as a small child, it is no surprise that they can't remember even farther back to recall what they did in a past life. This forgetfulness occurs even in those cultures where past lives are considered normal. Even in those cultures children are not always encouraged to speak out. Parents everywhere simply want their children to be obedient little people. Parents really have no desire for children to be former sophisticated adults.

So, even though as adults we do not hold these memories in our conscious minds they haven't disappeared from our subconscious

minds. Consequently, through the phenomenon of hypno-regressive therapy many adult patients have related past lives to their psychiatrists. This often occurs accidentally when they are
hypno-regressed for other reasons.

Now admittedly, a large portion of these reported past life memories from hypno-regressive therapy might merely be dreams and
wishes. Some psychologists working in this field believe that many
so-called *remembered past lives* may in fact be wishful thinking. There
always seem to be too many people remembering past lives as
Napoleon or Cleopatra, and few that remember a past life as Joe the
plumber, or Clyde the garbage collector. Yet, I don't want to throw
the baby out with the bath water by making a blanket condemnation
of the entire field of investigation due to a few spurious results.

On the other hand, I have also found numerous cases where the
patient under hypnosis does things they have no knowledge of in
this present life. For example, one patient remembers being a field
hand, and can also speak an extinct dialect of a foreign language
which they have never studied, while also explaining how to use
ancient farm tools not in common use for over a hundred years.
Such cases seem very conclusive of that soul having lived a prior life.

So, I listen to the wisdom of Dr. William James, former professor of
psychology at Harvard and a member of the American Society for
Psychical Research who said:

> **"To prove the hypothesis that not all crows are black, it
> only requires the finding of one white crow."**
>
> Dr. William James

Consequently, I appreciate the careful work of Dr. Brian Weise, an
M.D. Psychiatrist who accidentally regressed a patient into a prior life
during hypnotism. Upon awakening this patient had no memories of
the past life. Dr. Weise who had formerly been a skeptic, was intrigued
by his findings. So he regressed this same patient numerous additional times. Eventually, due to the portents of his own research Weise
himself became a believer in reincarnation and past lives.

Under hypnotic regression Dr. Weise's patients even have memories
of the time spent *between* lives as well as the progression of several
past lives. In his work Dr. Weise has held lengthy conversations in
real time with "Masters" who apparently are conscious beings, separate from the patient being regressed, and who act as guides or

guardian angels and seem to be tending to the patient's ongoing spiritual life. These "Masters" have told Dr. Weise, through the medium of the hypnotized patient's voice, things about the doctor himself that the patient did not know, and could not have known. Indeed, the "Masters" even told Dr. Weise that they told him these specific things, which the patient could not know, in order to approximate single blind conditions and show Dr. Weise that they were real and separate entities existing outside the consciousness of the patient and not a mental construction of the hypnotized patient.[24]

Both Dr. Weiss and Dr. Stevenson state that a healthy skepticism about all this is required when one investigates these fields, since it is an occult area where much misinformation is passed off as real, and where charlatans abound. But, every once in a while there are in fact a few *White Ravens*. *e*specially, with the rigorous scientific research methods which Dr. Ian Stevenson used to document those thousands of cases of children remembering past lives. So, let's look at the work of both Stevenson and Weise.

THE WORK OF Dr. IAN STEVENSON:

Dr. Stevenson has carried out lengthy investigations of over 3000 cases of children remembering past lives, in a study that has taken place over 50 years working in Eastern and Western cultures. Here are a few examples of the cases he has verified:

1. **BISHEN CHAND CASE**:[25,26,27] Bishen Chand Kapoor was born into the Gulham family in 1921 in Barielly, India. At the age of one and a half, he began asking questions about a town called Pilibhit, which was located about fifty miles away. A place no one in his family knew much about and they did not know anyone who lived there. Bishen asked his parents to take him there, and it was obvious to them that he believed he had lived there in a prior life. By the time Bishen was five years old he could clearly articulate memories of his former life and from that village where he and his family had never visited.

By 1926, he was stating that in the former life had been named Laxmi Narain, was the son of a wealthy landowner, and claimed to remember an uncle named Har Narain. Later, it would be discovered that this "uncle" was actually the father of Chand's remembered self with that same name of Laxmi. The young Chand described the house of Laxmi Narain, including various features of the layout, as well as a neighbor's house with a green gate, and how he had enjoyed the singing and dancing of the young women who entertained men in bars. He often spoke and could even read words of Urdu, a language written in Arabic script, even though Hindi was the language spoken in Chand's home and no one had taught him Urdu or how to read it.

> **Note** *These two items are remarkable, a mere five year old child remembering how he enjoyed watching the dancing girls in adult bars during his past life, and also speaking and reading a foreign language which he has not been taught.*

A local attorney, K.K.N. Sahay, heard about Chand's memories and came to the house to record statements from the boy and other family members. In one of those most surprising memories, the boy recounted killing a suitor of his mistress, **showing surprising awareness for a five year old of the difference between a wife and a mistress**. None of the family, nor the attorney had ever heard of the real Laxmi Narain. It is important to know that the attorney wrote down Chand's complete narrative at this time *before the attorney or Chand ever traveled to Pilibhit.*

When the attorney, along with the young Chand and Chand's father, traveled the fifty miles to Pilibhit, it was immediately confirmed that a man named Laxmi Narain had indeed shot and killed a rival lover of a prostitute who was still in the town. Narain had avoided prosecution because of his wealth, but had died two years later at age 32. By the time Chand was five not quite eight years had elapsed since the death of the adult Laxmi Narain.

When taken to Laxmi's old school, the boy ran to the classroom, described the teacher, and from an old photograph, identified and named classmates, one of whom was in the crowd that had gathered. Chand, had a heartwarming reunion with Laxmi's mother, whom he greatly preferred over his own biological mother. The green gate was seen as described, and when given Laxmi's tabla drums, he was reported to have played them with great skill. Before leaving the house Chand revealed where he had, during the past life as the adult Laxmi Narain, hidden some gold coins, which were recovered the following day.

This story clearly suggests that the consciousness survives in a very real form. The facts of Chand's language and musical skills, the adult emotions this toddler displayed, his identification of people by name from a photograph, even though he had never met them in this life, all are irrefutable proof that the consciousness survives. This case has been carefully verified and documented by the researchers at the University of Virginia. So it would appear that we have at least one WHITE RAVEN.

2. MARTA LORENZ CASE:[28] This is one of my personal favorites because it reads like a dramatic novella. But, it has been carefully researched, by Dr. Ian Stevensen and also because the return to the second life was "forecast" during the first life, the parents having been given the prediction before the birth wisely chose to observe the second life (their later daughter) under strict single blind laboratory conditions. The results of this decision provide amazing evidence. Here are the details as carefully documented by Dr. Ian Stevenson who has interviewed all the players except the original Sinha.

Maria Januaria de Oliviero, neck-named Sinha or Sinhazinha, was born about 1890, in the village of Dom Feliciano, about a hundred miles SW of Puerto Alegre in the province of Rio Grande de Sul, the westernmost state of Brazil. After Sinha's father disapproved of one of her suitors, the young man committed suicide. Sinha, who loved the young man, was distraught and so exposed herself to the elements and to tuberculosis, acquired an infection of the lungs and larynx, and then a few months later she also died.

However, on her death bed she acknowledged to her dear friend **Ida Lorenz** that she wanted to die and had tried to become infected with TB. Then she also promised Ida that she would return again and be born as ida's daughter. Sinha further predicted that:
"When reborn and at an age when I can speak on the mystery of rebirth in the body of the little girl who will be your daughter, I shall relate many things of my present life, and thus you will recognize the truth".

Sinha died the next day (in October 1917) just after her declaration to later return as Ida's daughter. At that time she had been about 28 years old.

Ten months later, on August 14, 1918, Ida Lorenz gave birth to a daughter, whom she named Marta. Ida and her husband had agreed to carefully never speak of Sinha's prediction to their other children, nor to the neighbors, or to anyone who might ever come in contact with any future daughters.

Well, in these dream-like visions of his, among those deceased persons whom he saw handled according to the diversity of their merits, he recognized also some whom he had known when alive. That they were the very persons themselves I might perchance have believed, had he not in the course of this seeming dream of his seen also some who are alive even to this present time, namely, some clerks of his district, by whose presbyter there he was told to be baptized at Hippo by me, which thing he said had also taken place. So then he had seen a presbyter, clerks, myself, persons, to wit, not yet dead, in this vision in which he afterwards also saw dead persons.....

After much that he saw, he narrated how he had, moreover, been led into Paradise, and how it was there said to him, when he was thence dismissed to return to his own family, "Go, be baptized, if thou wilt be in this place of the blessed." Thereupon, being admonished to be baptized by me, he said it was done already. He who was talking with him replied, "Go, be truly baptized; for that thou didst but see in the vision." After this he recovered, went his way to Hippo.

Easter was now approaching, he gave his name among the other Competents, alike with very many unknown to us; nor did he care to make known the vision to me or to any of our people. He was baptized, at the close of the holy days he returned to his own place. After the space of two years or more, I learned the whole matter; first, through a certain friend of mine and his at my own table, while we were talking about some such matters: then I took it up, and made the man in his own person tell me the story, in the presence of some honest townsmen of his attesting the same, both concerning his marvellous illness, how he lay all but dead for many days, and about that other Curma the smith, what I have mentioned above, and about all these matters; which, while he was telling me, they recalled to mind, and assured me, that they had also at that time heard them from his lips. Wherefore, just as he saw his own baptism, and myself, and Hippo, and the basilica, and the baptistery, not in the very realities, but in a sort of similitudes of the things; and so likewise certain other living persons, without consciousness on the part of the same living persons: then why not just so those dead persons also, without consciousness on the part of the same dead persons?

Here with Curma you have several "standard" items from the NDE:

1. Obviously Near-Death, his body did not respond to any stimuli
2. He is guided there by the grim reapers who have apparently gotten the wrong Curma.
3. He is told to return.
3. He was greeted by others already deceased.
4. He has obviously come back.

Note: Saint Augustine, revered doctor of the Christian faith, obviously believed these reports of the NDE. Consequently, for a modern day Christian theologian to say that the Christian church disbelieves the NDE, is simply naïve, and goes against St. Augustine..

CONCLUSION:

All of this shows that whether the organized church believes it is real or not the Near-Death experience is not a New Age fantasy, but has been with us for thousands of years.

CHAPTER 4

MEMORIES OF PAST LIVES

"...there are three claims in the ESP field which, in my opinion, deserve serious study... One of these is that young children some-times report the details of a previous life, which upon checking turn out to be accurate ....and which they could not have known about in any other way than reincarnation... "

the late Carl Sagan

"The transmigrations (reincarnation) of souls was taught for a long time among the early Christians as an esoteric and traditional doctrine which was to be divulged to only a small number of the elect."

Jerome (340-420AD) in a letter to Dimeterias

"I lay down my life that I may take it up again.......I have power to lay it down, and I have power to take it up again."

Jesus, quoted from John 10:17-18 (NIV)

"You should not be surprised at my saying, "You must be born again'

Jesus, quoted from John 3:7 (NIV)

"An incarnation comes an incarnation goes".
Qoheleth (Ecclesiastes) 1:4.translation according
to a second century Talmudic scholar[14]
"A generation comes a generation goes",
Ecclesiastes 1:4 (NIV) Translation according to
Christian Bible scholars

REINCARNATION and PAST LIFE REGRESSIONS:

If you were raised in the Western cultural perspective then you might well want to ask, "Do people really believe in reincarnation?" But, a Spring 2007 poll of Americans over 50 years old revealed that

23 percent of them believe in reincarnation, (meaning the re-birth of the consciousness in a new physical body), and in the Northeast United States the number rises to 31 percent. Also, the same study found that the baby boomers were even more likely to believe in reincarnation.

> Note: An earlier Gallup poll taken in October 2001,[15] found that among American adults 18 and over, 25% said they did in fact believe in reincarnation. Another 20% simply didn't know, 54% were sure they didn't believe in it and the remaining 1% had no opinion. At that time, belief was only slightly higher among males than females but it varied significantly between age groups. Belief in reincarnation among 28-29 year-olds was found to be 25%, among 30-49 year-olds 22%, and people 50 and over had the highest level of belief at 28%.

Suffice it to say that in the Western world one in four people believes in reincarnation.

MAJORITY OPINION: However, these poles were all taken in the Western world. Strikingly different is the opinion of the world population as a whole. Belief in the *Single Life Theory*, which is so prominent in the west, is actually a minority opinion when the whole world is considered. Most of the world, especially people in the far east believe instead that reincarnation is a fact as one researcher found;

> **"That's the paradox,...,** *"In the west people say, 'Why are you spending money to study reincarnation when we know it is impossible'. In the East they say, 'Why are you spending money to study reincarnation when we know it is a fact?"*[16]
> Dr. Ian Stevensen, University of Virginia researcher
> on children who remember past lives.

At first it might seem strange that the *Single Life Theory* is only believed in Europe, the Near East, and by the descendants of Europeans now living in North and South America. Yet, all of these people are descended only from ancestors who were once part of the Roman Empire. History explains that this *Single Life Theory* along with rejection of reincarnation was enforced upon them by their ancestors religions (Catholic, Protestant and Moslem) in the centuries after Roman emperor Justinian outlawed belief in multiple lifetimes in 553AD, and then used the power of the Roman church and the Roman legions to enforce his *Single Life Theory* throughout the empire by simply killing everyone who disagreed.

On the other hand, before Justinian decreed precisely what the Roman world would be allowed to believe, the majority of the ancient cultures inside the Roman Empire believed in reincarnation, just like the rest of the world still does today.

CHRISTIAN REINCARNATION: Further, Jesus, his disciples, Saint Paul and the early Christian fathers all believed in reincarnation and continued to do so for over 500 years after Christ's death.

Justin Martyr (100–165 A.D.) expressly stated that the soul inhabits more than one human body.[17]

Below is a quote from Origen (185 - 253 AD) the Christian bishop at Alexandria who during the third and early fourth century was respected by his fellow bishops as the foremost Christian scholar. Here is what the Origen said about reincarnation and karma:

> *Every soul...... comes into this world strengthened by the victories or weakened by the defeats of its previous life. Its place in this world as a vessel appointed to honor or dishonor is determined by its previous merits or demerits. Its work in this world determines its place in the world which is to follow this one.*[18]

Encyclopedia Britannica states that Origen was "the most prominent of all the Church Fathers with the possible exception of Augustine", while St. Jerome (347-420AD) at one time considered him as "the greatest teacher of the Church after the apostles". St. Gregory of Nyssa (335 – 394 AD) Bishop of Nyssa, speaking a hundred years later in the fourth century described Origen as, "*The prince of Christian Learning in the third century*".[19] And, here is what St. Gregory thought about karma and reincarnation:

> *"It is absolutely necessary that the soul should be healed and purified and that if it does not take place during this life on earth, it must be accomplished in future lives".*[20]

So, it is apparent that in the centuries before the Roman Emperors began to take over the church to use it as a political tool, that the early Christians Fathers (including Origen, Jerome and St. Gregory) did all believe in reincarnation.

NICENE CREED SUPPORTS REINCARNATION: For example, a short review of the language in the Nicene Creed shows that there is no statement which is not compatible with reincarnation. Further, the statement that Christ is "Light of Light" indicates that *the light* must be being seen somewhere (maybe in an NDE). *The light* is mostly only spoken of this way in the Gnostic texts:

Alan Hugenot

- *Jesus said, "It is I who am the light which is above them all, It is I who am the All"* Gospel of Thomas Verse 77
- *"If they say to you 'where did you come from?' Say to them, 'We came from The Light".* Gospel of Thomas, verse 50

Finally, the last statement in the Nicene creed, "I look for the resurrection of the dead and the life of the world to come", is much more easily interpreted as speaking about future lifetimes reincarnated in this physical world (world to come), than it is to try to twist its meaning into figuratively speaking of a future heaven, as a world to come! If, this statement was honestly intended to mean, "Heaven to come", then it should say "and the life of the heaven to come". Obviously, the authors chose "world", which means future worldly lifetimes, which goes along with the Christianity of Origen, Jerome and St. Gregory which includes reincarnation, and does not as easily support Justinian's single lifetime theology.

Note: The Nicene creed was supposedly originally written in 325 AD at the council of Nicea. It was supposedly then revised and adopted at Constantinople in 381AD. However, numerous early Christian scholars (Hort, Caspari, Harnack, and others) have found no evidence of its adoption at the 381AD council. These scholars are of the opinion that the Constantinopolitan form did not originate at the Council of Constantinople, because it is not in listed anywhere in the Acts (meeting minutes) of the council of 381.

Instead, they believe that it was inserted there at a later date. This is supported by the fact that St. Gregory who attended the 381 council, mentions only the Nicene formula adverting to its incompleteness about the Holy Ghost at the time of the 381 council. This clearly shows that he (one of the leading bishops of his time) did not know of the alleged Constantinopolitan form which satisfies this deficiency, and which was supposedly adopted at this council which he attended. Further, the writing of the Latin Fathers say nothing of this version of the creed before the middle of the fifth century (approx..450 AD), which is 70 years after the 381 council.

REJECTION OF ORIGEN: Unfortunately, beginning in 311 AD, some 60 years after Origen's death, and continuing for the following 240 years, critics of Origen and his doctrines of karma and reincarnation, who themselves subscribed to the one-life hypothesis began to attack him on individual points of theology. But, none of these critics ever provided a complete systematic theology which adequately opposed Origen or replaced his theology with any better explanation or ontology of the afterlife. Finally, Justinian decreed the official rejection of reincarnation in 553 AD and killed anyone who did not agree.

40

But, in order for this profound advancement to happen, many in both the scientific and religious communities must denounce their addiction to prejudiced, closed-minded, dogmatic beliefs (superstitions) and instead allow society to open its awareness to this new synthesis of understanding. Dr. Alexander believes that the progression of individual conscious awakening will cause this movement in society.

"One thing that we will have to let go of is this kind of addiction to simplistic, primitive reductive materialism because there's really no way that I can see a reductive materialist model coming remotely in the right ballpark to explain what we really know about consciousness now.

"having been through my coma, I can tell you that's exactly wrong and that in fact the mind and consciousness are independent of the brain. It's very hard to explain that, certainly if you're limiting yourself to that reductive materialist view." Quote from Dr. Eben Alexander III

Due to his lifetime spent studying neuroscience, Dr. Alexander's near-death experience provides dramatic proof of the reality of the afterlife. His website is http://www.lifebeyonddeath.net/ Also, You can watch a short video narrated by Morgan Freeman, which describes Dr. Eben Alexander's NDE at http://www.youtube.com/watch?feature=player_embedded&v=4qUGV4n23dY[11]

ANCIENT NEAR DEATH ACCOUNTS
Also, none of this is new science, the history of Near-Death Experiences in the recorded literature goes back several thousand years throughout the surviving literature of the ancients back to at least 1000 BC. I will only review four of these which were recorded by well-known authors between 1000 BC and 400 AD.

JOB 1000 BC (Torah)	PERPETUA & SATURUS – 203AD (St. Augustine)
ER – 400 BC (Plato)	CURMA – 428 AD (St. Augustine)

It is interesting to note that two of these accounts come from the Roman Catholic father Saint Augustine, and that Job's account of his NDE reads very differently in several ancient Hebrew texts, than it does in the current edition of the New International Version (NIV) of the protestant Bible.

Approx. 1000 BC – JOB:

This narrative is related by the writer of the book of job, which most scholars believe was written sometime after the reign of Solomon and prior to the first exile of the Hebrews (Babylonian Captivity), this means it could have been written as early as 931 BC and as late as 597 BC. But, the events in Job's lifetime took place sometime between 2000 and 1000 BC, and most likely nearer to 1000 BC, having been transmitted *orally* prior to being written (which of course allows for great distortions to have inadvertently crept in).

The following verses from the NIV version of Job are a favorite of mine and also many other Christians. Often quoted on Easter Sunday, they come from the Hebrew of the old testament.

"I know that my Redeemer lives, and that in the end he will *stand upon the earth.* **And after my skin has been destroyed, Yet,** *in* **my flesh I will see God. I myself will see him with my own eyes – I and not another – How my heart yearns within me."**

Job 19:25-27 (NIV – text as printed)

But, several ancient Hebrew texts for these same verses provide alternative translations. Naturally, the NIV translators have chosen those translations that fit their chosen dogma of, "resurrection of the physical body". Yet, when I examined the alternative texts, which the NIV mentions in the foot notes, I found that those alternative versions actually agree in all details with what NDE has been reporting for thousands of years.

When I worked out the alternative translation I found that it contains no resurrection of the physical body but only resurrection of the spirit. Here is how the alternative Hebrew text reads

"I know that my Redeemer lives, and that in the end he will stand upon my grave. After I awake, though this body has been destroyed, then (while) yet apart from my flesh (i.e. out-of-body), I will see God. I myself will see him with my own eyes – I and not another – How my heart yearns within me."

Job 19:25-27 (NIV - Alternative Hebrew texts, as listed in NIV foot notes)

DID JOB HAVE AN NDE: This alternative translation shows clearly that Job is describing what he learned during an NDE. Certainly, all the conditions for an NDE were present for him. Earlier in the book Job's aliments are described.

- He is very sick,
- His entire body is covered with boils and
- He has wasted away to skin and bones.

In such condition he might as well be dead. So, while the details of his disease are sketchy, it is obvious that he has come very close to death (i.e Near-Death proximity) from this disease. Knowing that an NDE was probable, and seeing that what Job relates in the above verses 25-27 is the same gnosis which Near-Death survivors return with, it appears most probable that Job had an actual NDE and achieved the gnosis which derives from it prior to relating these verses. This is evident from the several "standard" items of the NDE gnosis which he shares here:

1. He knows that after death he will be *out-of-body*..... "apart from my flesh".
2. He knows his body will be destroyed, but he will still live on without it
3. He describes the experiencs much as it has been described in the NDE reports "apart from my flesh I will see God, I myself will see God with my own eyes".
4. He knows he will see *the light* (see God).
5. He knows that he has eternal life and cannot wait to get back there.

Further, Job's remark; "If a man die, shall he live again? All the days of my appointed time will I wait, till my change come." (Job 14:14, NIV) reminds me of my own NDE impression that, "Yet, a little while, and you can return to the Light".

Approx. 400 BC – Er: Related by Plato (428/427 BC – 348/347 BC),

THE NEAR-DEATH EXPERIENCE OF THE GREEK WARRIOR ER: Here is a report of a Near-Death experience which took place some 430 years before Saint Paul's NDE. This report is taken from Plato's Republic Vol. X, 614b, but this version is my on shortened paraphrase based on several descriptions appearing in multiple translations of Plato.[12]

> *Er, was a Greek warrior, the son of Armenius of Pamphylia, who was slain on the battlefield. His countrymen collected the corpses, and hauled them home in carts about the tenth day after the battle. Many of the bodies were already decayed. But, his body was still intact and was laid with the others on the funeral pyre to be burned about two days later, about twelve days after the battle. It*

was there after being counted dead for 12 days that Er came back to this life. Er then described what he had seen in the realms beyond.

*First, he said that his soul left his body (out of body). Next, he traveled with many other spirits to a place where there were two openings leading from earth into the afterlife. Between these openings sat some sort of divine beings. Apparently, the divine beings could see at a glance in some sort of display all the things that the soul had done while in its earthly life (**i.e life review - weighing of the heart**). After every judgment the divine beings told the righteous to go to the right and then upward to heaven. As they did this they attached a token to the souls representing the judgment which had been passed about their life review (**Ankh, or Key of Life**). Others were directed to the left and then downward (**directed to travel through the underworld**).*

All of what Er describes is represented in the ancient Egyptian weighing of the heart, when the soul with a heavy heart is directed to the underworld to be lead by Anuket to later be born again in a new body, and the righteous is given the key of life and directed to ascend into the heavens. (see chapter 7)

*However, the divine beings told Er that **he was to return and inform men** in the physical world about what the other world was like.*

NOTE: All modern Near-Death survivors, remember being told that it was **not yet their time**, and that **they must return to accomplish unfinished business.**

Most Near Death survivors interpret what they see in the perspective of their own religious cultural upbringing; Er was no doubt a Platonist who died about 400 years before the Christian era. What we have in Plato's narrative is Er's interpretation of what he saw colored in the light of his prior religious beliefs. Regardless of that, the reported experience was almost exactly the same as every other reported NDE throughout history right up to today.

NDE Research has shown that everyone, myself, Saint Paul, Er and all other Near-Death survivors from many different religions and cultures all report the same events. They may interpret its meaning differently depending on their different religious backgrounds, but they all report some or all of the same basic events, as itemized in this list taken from, P.H.M. Atwater's 1988 book *Coming Back to Life.*

1. A feeling of floating out of their body
2. Passing through a darkness or tunnel
3. Ascending toward a light at the end of the tunnel.
4. Greeted by friendly voices, people or beings.
5. The life review, or seeing a panoramic view of the life just lived, with assessment of the meaning of the events. (*The weighing of the heart*)
6. A reluctance to return to the earth plane
7. Warped sense of time and space while over there
8. Disappointment at being revived.

Approx. 203 AD - PERPETUA & SATURUS:

Related by Saint Augustine (354 – 430 AD)

And I asked, and this was what was shown me. I saw a golden ladder of marvelous height, reaching up even to heaven, and very narrow, so that persons could only ascend it one by one; and on the sides of the ladder was fixed every kind of iron weapon. There were there swords, lances, hooks, daggers; so that if any one went up carelessly, or not looking upwards, he would be torn to pieces and his flesh would cleave to the iron weapons. And under the ladder itself was crouching a dragon of wonderful size, who lay in wait for those who ascended, and frightened them from the ascent. And Saturus went up first, who had subsequently delivered himself up freely on our account, not having been present at the time that we were taken prisoners. And he attained the top of the ladder, and turned towards me, and said to me, Perpetua, I am waiting for you; but be careful that the dragon does not bite you.' And I said, 'In the name of the Lord Jesus Christ, he shall not hurt me.' And from under the ladder itself, as if in fear of me, he slowly lifted up his head; and as I trod upon the first step, I trod upon his head. And I went up, and I saw an immense extent of garden, and in the midst of the garden a white-haired man sitting in the dress of a shepherd, of a large stature, milking sheep; and standing around were many thousand white-robed ones. And he raised his head, and looked upon me, and said to me, 'Thou are welcome, daughter.' And he called me, and from the cheese as he was milking he gave me as it were a little cake, and I received it with folded hands; and I ate it, and all who stood around said *Amen*. And at the sound of their voices I was awakened, still tasting a sweetness which I cannot describe. And I immediately related this to my brother, and we understood that it was to be a passion, and we ceased henceforth to have any hope in this world.

Here with Perpetua and Saturus you have several "standard" items from the NDE:

1. They are guided up to the afterlife confronted with a ladder to climb.
2. They meet with a Good Shepherd (being of light) who does not identify himself.
3. They no longer place their hope in this world, but wait to go to that one.
4. They have obviously come back.

Approx. 428 AD- CURMA:

Related by Saint Augustine (354 – 430 AD)[13] This is also taken from his <u>Retractions</u> published two years prior to his death where he tried to clarify all the mis-intrepretations the Roman Catholics had made from his writing.

A certain man by name Curma, of the municipal town of Tullium, which is hard by Hippo…. being ill, and all his senses entranced, lay all but dead for several days: a very slight breathing in his nostrils, which on applying the hand was just felt, and barely betokened that he lived, was all that kept him from being buried for dead. Not a limb did he stir, nothing did he take in the way of sustenance, neither in the eyes nor in any other bodily sense was he sensible of any annoyance that impinged upon them.

Yet he was seeing many things like as in a dream, which, when at last after a great many days he woke up, he told that he had seen. And first, presently after he opened his eyes, Let someone go, said he, to the house of Curma the smith, and see what is doing there. And when someone had gone thither, the smith was found to have died in that moment that the other had come back to his senses, and, it might almost be said, revived from death.

When, as those who stood by eagerly listened, he told them how the other had been ordered to be taken up, when he himself was dismissed; and that he had heard it said in that place from which he had returned, that it was not Curma of the Curia, but Curma the smith who had been ordered to be fetched to that place of the dead.

part of one connected soul, although the consciousness seems to individuate on both sides of the veil.

6. **I no longer believe in retribution after death**, nor a heaven or hell as taught by most western religions. I understood that there is only something to be learned in this physical life, and that any judgment we make after death, during our life review, is that, "it was all good".

7. **I also knew that no one leaves this physical life until their time**, which is not measured as a date, but as a condition of learning, they go when they are finished with learning. Not one second early, nor one second late.

THE DIFFICULTY OF EXPLAINING ALL THIS: Waking up and finding myself back in the physical world I immediately wanted to share what I had discovered about the afterlife and consciousness survival, and especially share with others how free that gnosis made me.

I had been gifted by the universe with the most precious piece of knowledge mankind, here in the physical plane, can ever have... that life continues after physical death....., but I quickly found that nobody wanted to hear about it!

I knew that eternal life was real, that there is also no hell to pay, and that our consciousness survives in an alternative dimension. I also knew that eternal life was *not something earned down at the church, but was a free gift for everyone,* precisely as St. Paul had declared in Ephesians:

"For it is by Grace you have been saved ..... it is the gift of God, not of works so that no one can boast.[6] St. Paul's letter to the Ephesians 2:6-9 (NIV)

MEDICAL COMMUNITY DOES NOT WANT TO HEAR ME: Immediately after coming back here, when I began to describe my experience, the nurses quickly hushed me up on this subject. They feared for my safety. This was back in 1970 five years before the Near-Death experience began to reach the mainstream of medicine. At the time, many nurses knew about this phenomenon, but doctors were still refusing to think about it. Doctors who refused to consider it as real believed the NDE was merely hallucinations. Psychiatrists wanted to condemn it as a psychotic disorder and were anxious to commit anyone who persisted in talking about it to an asylum. So, I quickly learned to keep quiet about it while in the hospital.

MINISTERS REFUSE TO HEAR IT ALSO: After leaving the hospital I hoped to discuss my experience with religious leaders, believing that would be a safer context and that the pastor would listen to me without trying to commit me to the asylum. But, when I spoke with them they also told me it was merely an hallucination or a dream, because it disagreed with their *particular* interpretation of scriptures and so could not possibly be true.

I was shocked by their desire to remain ignorant on the subject. Here, I had the proof of the afterlife which the church had been seeking for two thousand years. Yet, because my details were slightly different from their adopted speculations they wanted to reject it.

My family also had great difficulties with it. Out of loyalty to me they wanted to believe me, but found it hard to step away from what they had believed for so long.

THE "STANDARD" NEAR-DEATH EXPERIENCE: In 1975 five years after I had my NDE Dr. Raymond Moody, M.D. published the results of his study of NDE's in a book entitled *Life After Life*.[7] He had studied hundreds of Near-Death experiences and analyzed the collated results. In that text he described what he had found to be the "standard" near death experience. He noted that most experiencers did not recall the whole sequence, but all had the majority of the parts. Here is what Dr. Moody reported:

> *A man is dying, and as he reaches the point of greatest physical distress, he hears himself pronounced dead by his doctor. He begins to hear an uncomfortable noise, a loud ringing or buzzing, and at the same time feels himself moving very rapidly through a long dark tunnel. After this, he suddenly finds himself outside of his own physical body, but still in the immediate physical environment, and he sees his own body from a distance, as though he is a spectator. He watches the resuscitation attempt from this unusual vantage point and is in a state of emotional upheaval.*

> *After a while, he collects himself and becomes more accustomed to his odd condition. He notices that he still has a "body", but one of a very different nature and with very different powers from the physical body he has left behind. Soon other things begin to happen. Others come to meet and to help him. He glimpses the spirits of relatives and friends who have already died, and a loving warm spirit of a kind he has never encountered before, **a being of light appears before him. This being asks him a question, non-verbally,** to make him evaluate his life and helps him along by showing him a panoramic, instantaneous playback of the major*

events of his life. (This is the life review or **weighing of the heart***) At some point he finds himself approaching some sort of barrier or border apparently representing the limit between earthly life and the next life.* **Yet, he finds that he must go back to the earth, that the time for his death has not yet come. At this point he resists, for by now he is taken up with his experience in the afterlife and does not want to return,** *He is overwhelmed by intensive feelings of joy, love and peace. Despite his attitude, though, he somehow reunites with his physical body and lives.*

Later, he tries to tell others, but he has trouble doing so. In the first place, he can find no human words adequate to describe these unearthly episodes. He also finds that others scoff, **so he stops telling other people.** *Still, the experience affects his life profoundly, especially his views about death and his relationship to life*[8] *(annotations in parenthesis are authors)*

THE LIFE REVIEW:

The life review which is a standard element that occurs in many Near-Death experiences is uncannily similar to *the weighing of the heart,* depicted in the ancient Egyptian papyrus of *La Pesee du Coeur* (see chapter 7). And, during many NDE's this is the point at which the consciousness makes the decision to return to life after reviewing the emotions of their own heart. This event in the modern NDE agrees with the ancient Egyptian myth where, if your heart is not lighter than a feather, but is still burdened with the cares of this life, then you must return to the physical life. Following are two descriptions of the life review from modern NDE experiencers interviewed by Kenneth Ring.

1971 AD - BELLE'S NDE reported by Kenneth Ring in his 1984 book *Heading Toward Omega.*

"You are shown your life—and **you do the judging.** *Had you done what you should do? You think. 'Oh, I gave six dollars to someone that didn't have much and that was great of me., That didn't mean a thing. It's the little things—maybe a hurt child that you helped or just to stop and say hello to a shut-in. Those are the things that are most important....You are judging yourself. You have been forgiven all your sins, but are you able to forgive yourself for not doing all the things you should have done and some little cheaty things that maybe you've done in life.* **Can you forgive yourself? This is the judgment.**

1971 AD - DARRYL'S NDE reported by Kenneth Ring also in *Heading Toward Omega*.

> *"As the light came toward me, it came to be a person—yet it wasn't a person. It was a being that radiated. And inside this radiant luminous light which had a silver tint to it—white, with a silver tint—was what looked to be a man......Now, I didn't know exactly who it was, you know, but it was the first person that showed up and I had this feeling that the closer this light got to me the more awesome and pure this love –this feeling that I would call love... And this person said, "Do you know where you are?" I never got a chance to answer that question, for all of a sudden—"my life passed before me". But, it was not my life that passed before me nor was it a three-dimensional caricature of the events in my life. **What occurred was every emotion I have ever felt in my life,** I felt. And my eyes were showing me the basis of how that emotion affected my life. What my life had done so far to affect other people's lives using the feeling of pure love that was surrounding me as the point of comparison....**Looking' at yourself from the point of how much love you have spread to other people is devastating'. You will never get over it. I am six years away from that day (the day of the NDE) and I am not over it yet.***

RESEARCH IT FOR MYSELF: Lacking any support from the medical community or the church I began to do my own research on the subject. Eventually, I found St. Paul's description of his own Near-Death experience in 2nd Corinthians 12 (as quoted below). Saint Paul describes his own NDE, which occurred during the decade after Jesus death (about 35 AD), St. Paul is here speaking about his own conversion experience on the road to Damascus, and when he saw the light, but doing so in the third person, and he clearly is speaking about an *out-of-body* experience. When the same story is related by Luke in the book of Acts, the being of light that St. Paul is supposedly speaking to on the road to Damascus is identified by Luke as Jesus, but, in St. Paul's own telling of the story in 2nd Corinthians he himself does not identify Jesus.

> *"I must go on boasting. Although there is nothing to be gained, I will go on to visions and revelations from the Lord. I know a man in Christ, who fourteen years ago was caught up to the third heaven. Whether it was in the body or out of the body, I do not know – God knows. And I know that this man, whether in the body or apart from the body I do not know, but God knows, was caught up to paradise. He heard inexpressible*

things, things that man is not permitted to tell. I will boast about a man like that, but I will not boast about myself, except about my weaknesses. Even if I should choose to boast, I would not be a fool, because I would be speaking the truth. But I refrain, so no one will think more of me than is warranted by what I do or say. [9] St Paul's second letter to Corinthians 12:1-5 (NIV)

Saint Paul describes that he went out-of-body and "heard inexpressible things" just as happens in the modern NDE narratives where the experiencer travels out-of-body to commune with *the light*, and finds it to be ineffable.

For me, this was concrete evidence that I was not alone. Now, I knew that this revered apostle Saint Paul, a great Christian had also "been there" with *the light*, just as I had. This changed my opinion of him and I then began to study the *real* Saint Paul. No longer would I study him from the *proper* perspective of the Roman church and its prodigal child the Protestant church, but instead from the perspective of a fellow Near-Death survivor.

FINDING TOOLS FOR LIVING IN THIS WORLD: Now, with a new understanding of St. Paul I searched further in the scriptures and found the following statement in 1st Corinthians, which gave me a tool that I now use to find direction in life.

My message and my preaching were not with wise and persuasive words, but with a **demonstration of the Spirit's power, so that your faith might not rest on men's wisdom,** *but on God's power.*

1 Corinthians 2:4-5 (NIV).

Here Saint Paul was describing a tool of the faith that all Christian believers should use in their own lives. St. Paul was clearly telling me and all Christian believers that,

"We should not rely on the words of men and their interpretation,"

Instead St. Paul wants us to,

"Rely only on what the Spirit reveals to us personally in our own heart".

Saint Paul, right there in the NIV was advising us to believe only the Gnosis of our own hearts and not what some learned church leader is telling us, if it goes against our own heart. Obviously, Paul was a

Gnostic Christian rather than the limited type of believer that later became the only allowable "orthodoxy" on punishment of death.

CONVICTION THAT THE CONSCIOUSNESS SURVIVES:

All NDE survivors seem to have arrived at the same conclusion, that the individual consciousness definitely survives death, and this brings them great peace. This is the gnosis in their hearts.

1958 AD - NDE OF CARROL PARRISH-HARRA: This woman makes the clearest statement of what each NDE survivor believes about death:

> *"Being in that magnificent presence, I understood it all. I realized that consciousness is life. We will live in and through much, but **this consciousness we know that is behind our personality will continue.** I knew now that the purpose of life does not depend on me; it has its own purpose. I realized that the flow of it will continue even as I will continue. New serenity entered my being".*[10]

Today, 50 years later the NDE experience still delivers the same conclusions. Here is what an M.D. Neurosurgeon and Harvard Medical professor found during his own NDE in 2008.

2008 AD - A NEUROSURGEON HAS A NEAR DEATH EXPERIENCE: In November 2008 Dr. Eben Alexander III, a renowned neurosurgeon and Harvard professor, who had spent 54 years believing in the generally accepted materialist scientific worldview, had a Near-Death experience. Previously, Dr. Alexander thought that as a neurosurgeon he knew how the brain and mind worked. But, after this experience in which he spent a week in a coma he changed his viewpoint completely.

> *NOTE: Dr. Alexander suffered a prolonged case of severe bacterial meningitis. This disease, because of its selective destruction of the outer surface, or "neocortex" of the brain is usually fatal. Virtually no one who is comatose for a week due to such acute bacterial meningitis survives.*

Shocked by the hyper-reality that he experienced, which many had reported in NDEs, Dr. Alexander has spent the following two and a half years reconciling his experience with contemporary physics and cosmology. He finds that his spiritual experience (or NDE) is *totally consistent with the leading edges of scientific understanding today.* Dr. Alexander believes that taken together science and spirituality will thrive in a new symbiosis offering the most profound insight into fundamental Truth, and I believe he is entirely correct.

commuted from the university campus out to my job in West Eugene.

Up until that time I had always been a pretty normal American. My family attended Protestant services on Sundays, I liked hiking and camping with the Boy Scouts. I got good grades in history math and science. I had joined the Navy went to boot camp in San Diego, learned ship navigation at Quartermaster's school in Newport, Rhode Island, and enjoyed navigating my destroyer to foreign ports during the Vietnam war, before returning home to start college.

My life up to that point had been mostly concerned with finding a career, getting a date, being accepted at a college, paying for it, etc. Consequently, any questions about what happens after death and whether our consciousness survives were pushed aside. I easily accepted the prevailing Western cultural philosophy that we live only one life, and if asked what I believed came after death I would have said, **"According to my church we go to heaven or hell, but I'm not actually sure what really happens"**. At that stage of my life there were many more pressing problems to solve and thoughts of the afterlife could wait.

But, everything changed on the evening of May 27, 1970. I was riding my motorcycle back to the University of Oregon campus on the way home from my design job, when I was involved in a collision with a car. I was severely injured and rushed by ambulance to the intensive care unit at Sacred Heart General Hospital, Eugene, Oregon, where I was hospitalized for about 33 days.

My right femur (thigh bone) was shattered, a portion of my right wrist (radius) was broken off and had lodged near my elbow, my right knee cap was completely crushed, and my head had experienced extreme trauma in a violent battering. My upper teeth had been destroyed entirely on one side of my jaw, and there were numerous fissures in my scull above the upper teeth caused when my open mouth and skull collided with the luggage rack on the car which I had the collision with.

When I arrived in the ER my condition was *critical,* but I had been stabilized and was not hemorrhaging, so they began preparing me for surgery. However, just prior to surgery I became incoherent and unconscious. Fearing that they might induce a permanent coma if they administered anesthesia the doctors postponed the surgery.

Later, after I had regained consciousness they waited three days before performing the surgery.

To this day, I recall nothing about the accident or arriving in the ER. My first recollections after the accident were when I awoke, out-of-body, on the other side in communion with *the being of Light*. I have no recollection of certain phases of leaving my body as described by other NDE survivors, but, I vividly recall returning into the physical body. Surprisingly, not many NDE narrations describe the return to the body except to say, "Suddenly, I was back in my body". Yet, I remember the details of this re-entry into physical matter in very clear visceral detail.

THE OTHER SIDE OF THE VEIL: The odyssey began for me when I just "woke up" on the other side, with *the being of light*. The feeling was as if I had always been there. I felt completely "home" at last. *The being of light* was an old friend who had known me for eons. Time itself had ceased, there was no schedule and no hurry. Dimensional space (3-D as we know it here in physical reality) was not a concept in effect there. Borders and boundaries did not seem to exist in any concrete way. I felt loved, at peace, and as if I was being held like a babe-in-arms. Yet, I knew from deep within me that I was connected to, and an integral part of, *the being of light* itself. We were not separate beings. Instead, I was one essence with the brilliant golden white *light*. Everything was more than O.K. I knew that I had been there for quite a while prior to waking up. I was aware that I had been being lovingly nurtured and I awoke feeling "restored".

Now, slowly I became aware that I must return to physical life in time and space (i.e. move back into the light energy of 3-D). This idea, that I must go back into matter and a physical body, came to me not in words but intuitively, from *the being of light*. What I received was a distinct impression (ESP), which communicated that,

> *"Yet, a little while, and you can return to the Light, but for now you must return to the physical life".*

This awareness, that things were not yet finished with my prior physical life on earth, was the natural result of the things we (the light and I) had been reviewing just before my full awakening to my presence with *the light*. I was aware that this return to physical life would only be *short term*, and I would soon be able to return home again to the light. So far, this short term assignment has been over 40 years, but still it remains for me only a temporary assignment before I will return to my true home with the light.

I noticed that *the light*, who I knew was connected with the supreme consciousness of the universe, did not bother to identify itself as being Jesus, God, nor any other name. I just knew that while I was there, *the light* was part of me and of all things, and that we knew each other intimately so there was no need for introductions or identity descriptions, we were part of each other, always had been and what could be more simple? I had never experienced such a state of connectedness or love. Many years later in my research I would find the clearest description of this state of being a part of everything in the universe in the following passage taken from the Gnostic Gospel of Phillip:

> *"It is not possible for anyone to see anything of the things that actually exist unless he becomes like them. This is not the way with man in the (physical) world: he sees the sun without being a sun; and he sees the heaven and the earth and all other things, but he is not these things. This is quite in keeping with the truth.*
>
> *But, (when) you saw something of that place (eternity), you became those things. (When) you saw the Spirit, you became Spirit. (When) you saw Christ, you became Christ. You saw the Father, (and) you shall become Father. So in this place (time and space) you see everything and do not see yourself, but in that place (eternity) you do see yourself and what you see you shall become".[3]*

Gospel of Phillip, (Nag Hammadi Library Codex II Tractate 3 p.61)
Interpretations in parenthesis are the author's

These words say it all. *"You did see yourself in that place and what you saw you shall become".*

MY RETURN TO THE BODY: Now, as I headed back to the physical life and reentering the feelings, pain and suffering of a physical body, *the being of light*, slowly began to be obscured by tendrils of reddish purple "blood", which began to wash over my view of *the light*. *The light* itself had now faded to an orange "sunset sky" behind a tie-died batik curtain of red tendrils. Slowly the red-purple tie-dyed streaks closing out the view of the golden orange sky thickened until the light was entirely obscured by the red-purple veil.

Note: all these colors were written down by me in the months following the NDE, yet I would find later in the Tibetan Book of the Dead the exact same colors being described as occurring in reverse order as one leaves the body just after the death of the physical body.

In a metaphorical sense, I speak of this as a lowering of a, "veil of blood and tears", believing that it represented the separation zone between the spiritual existence and the physical reality.

Many years later I would find the following passage in *A Course in Miracles* which is clearly describing that same veil:

"In the holy instant nothing happens that has not always been. Only the veil that has been drawn across reality is lifted. Nothing has changed. Yet the awareness of changelessness comes swiftly as the veil of time is pushed aside. No one, who has not yet experienced the lifting of the veil, and felt himself drawn irresistibly into the light behind it, can have faith in love without fear. Yet the Holy Spirit gives you this faith."[4]

A Course in Miracles, Chapter 5, Section VI (1977)

Being left alone again without *the light* was now uncomfortable, and *I truly did not want to come back here to this physical life.*

However, subjugating my "will" into the "blood" of this temporal existence I did came back into the flesh. I re-occupied my body and the process of re-entry caused excruciating pain. I believe this pain was not from my injuries, but was entirely due to the conversion from spirit to physical. It was painful as I "slammed" back into the confinement of a body holding feelings. I could feel the dense heaviness of the body's physical mass, and the pain of having nerves, feelings and emotions again, the literal thickness of the blood of existence, the hulking dense mass of physicality. These tangible feelings and the associated pain were all absent while I was with *the light*, only love and knowledge remained with me there. Communing with *the light* only "metaphysics" existed, but when I returned to time and space, I re-entered "physics", the polarization of material existence.

During this re-entry, just prior to *slamming* into the physical I saw myself surrounded by what I call **candle flames, or sparklers of light**. Later I would read, P.H.M. Atwater, another Near-Death survivor who records that,

"I floated ever so gently back into her body, moving as I went on **a layer of large bright sparklers** *such as those used on the Fourth of July"*[5]

Note: Notice how she speaks of her physical body in the third person.

Apparently, from her description, she also saw the same candle flames (sparklers) that I saw. Later in my research I would find that Thoth-Hermes in the ancient Egyptian records had stated that our soul is **sheathed in flames**. I also found that the first through fourth century Gnostic Christians and the Hellenistic Mystery religions prior to them, all called this flame filled reentry the "Baptism by Fire". It occurred for them after achieving enlightenment through an out-of-body spiritual communion with *the Light*. This "Baptism by Fire", marked the "Gnostic" level of "enlightenment" derived from literally "seeing the light".

> *Note: It isn't surprising that the original Gnostic Christianity often makes more sense to NDE survivors, while current versions of organized Christianity may seem to be all to weak, controlled, and watered down misinterpretations.*

THE BRAIN SHIFT: It was just like that, lying there at peace in atonement with the light and the universe, with not a care, and then suddenly "in the twinkling of an eye" re-entry into the intense pain and feeling of time and space.

Yet, I did not come back as the same guy at all. I had undergone an extreme psychological make over. The change that took place in my personality is described by many Near-Death survivors as being a *brain shift*. When you return to this life you are still a regular person, you haven't suddenly become a spiritual guru or shaman, although you may become one later. On-the-other hand, everything in your paradigm has shifted and you possess a rare gnosis that life is continuous.

It is as if your brain had disconnected like an unplugged computer. The brain had temporarily shut down and now the read only memory (ROM) is still there, but the random access memory, and anything held temporarily on it, has been wiped clean.

You have returned to re-energize the body's circuits (hardware) and begin to reboot the software, but it will never be as it was before. This return to the prior life is actually a second life and not at all a part of the first life, For me, personally, it took many years to overcome the expectations of friends and relatives who still saw me as being the prior personality, and whenever I would act differently from their expectations they would wonder what had come over me. They, even to this day do not realize that, although I am the same spirit yet I am a different personality than the one that died earlier. It is a better approximation to simply say that I was *reborn to a new life* (reincarnated) in the same body.

Alan Hugenot

Note: NDE survivors have actually done what most "born again" Christians only claim to have done........been born a second time into the same body...... This is what both Jesus and Saint Paul were actually talking about, where the old person has died and a new person is living there instead.

The past life was over, and I now had a new life. The medical professionals may say that I revived, or never even died. But, my memories of that prior life back in B.C (before crash) are somewhat dim and to describe them I like to say they are recorded in black and white. To recall those memories of that first life I have to go search them up in old files, which then have to be unzipped before I can access those dusty ROMs (read only memories). On the other hand, everything that has happened in this second life is held in RAM (random access memory) and is recalled immediately in vivid living color.

The altered world view and the psychological changes which also came back with me are listed below:

1. **I have no fear of dying.** While I do fear being injured or broken I simply have no fear of death itself. I know that death is only a transition and I am fully aware that our consciousness survives that change. I have only returned here again, "for a little while", and then I can return to the light. I also know that to my home with the light is where I will go when I leave the physical existence.

2. **Material things have almost completely lost their importance to me.** I am still a very responsible worker who pays his bills and maintains good credit with the banks. But, I am much more motivated by spiritual things rather than by materialism or success. People want me to worry about money, retirement, health insurance, wearing a seat belt, etc. I simply don't have deep concerns about these things. I am motivated to wear seat belts because it makes others happy, but sometimes I get ticketed because I don't remember to buckle up when driving alone.

3. **I am much more feeling, psychic, able to read others feelings and express love easily.** Many psychic experiences have continually been observed by me merely because of my changed perspective.

4. **I realize all the world's religions don't have it quite right** when it comes to dying. But, also that each is founded on the honorable principle of attempting to find "the way". Unfortunately, each religion has this unfounded notion that there is only one right way and, of course, they each believe it must be the one way they cooked up after a great deal of speculation. But, to prove that they are "right" they must find everyone else to be wrong. This quickly changes to "Kill the infidel".

5. **I no longer see any need for individual souls,** I felt a greater empathy for all souls. Later, I revisited this impression and realized that I actually see only one soul, which manifests itself in the physical world in many different egos, but, spiritually we are all

22

teenage boy who loved beer, green peppers and chicken nuggets, in fact when he had died in a motorcycle crash, he actually had chicken nuggets in his jacket pocket. This interesting concept, that the feelings and emotions are concepts of the flesh itself and stay with the physical material, is well documented by the Near Death experience, after death communications, and past life memories. But, the expose of that material is another story for a later book.

THIRD CAR FACT: Many people living in major cities do not own cars, and continue to have perfectly normal lives while living a totally 'OUT OF CAR" experience.

SIMILAR CARCASS FACT: Thousands of people report "OUT OF BODY" experiences where they continued to live while on the outside of their bodies.

I am one of those people who survived my own death, in which I also had an "OUT OF BODY" experience, and then returned to re-occupy (reincarnate in) the same physical body. I know from that personal experience that our cultural identification with our physical body as being the "real" us, is a complete and entire misconception, foisted onto us by the materialist thinking of both Newtonian science and the medieval church.

FOURTH CAR FACT: Many folks have owned several different cars.

SIMILAR CARCASS FACT: Thousands of mature souls have occupied several different carcasses. Researchers at the University of Virginia have documented thousands of cases of small children who remember their prior lives. The researchers have often been able to find the former relatives of the remembered prior life, and then verify the facts that the child, who is now occupying a new body, still remembers about the prior life which was lived in a different physical body. In several instances the researchers have documented and verified cases where a single soul will correctly remember having occupied more than one body in a series of several sequential lifetimes. Indeed, the literature produced on these studies by the late Dr. Ian Stevenson (who died in 2007) is fascinating reading. His associates are today continuing this research which is more fully described in chapter 4.

OBVIOUS BUT UNCOMFORTABLE CONCLUSIONS:

It is easy to see from this series of carcass facts, that the physical body is actually not the real "us" at all. In fact, it is quite obvious, and the only rational conclusion, that we are only the *operator* of that body. Further, these facts show that not only *can* we change bodies, we *do* change them.

MY BEST ADVICE: For many people this entire idea will be very uncomfortable, or downright disorienting because it goes against everything we have been taught. At first, this radical idea may seem to be turning your entire world upside down, but I do understand because I have been there myself.

Immediately after my own Near-Death experience I was disoriented and confused. The out-of- body experience of which it consisted was totally new to my experience, and went against everything I held as basic truths. Sure, I knew in undeniable detail what I had experienced. But, it quite disagreed with everything I had held dear up until that moment. It contradicted my religion (conservative Lutheran), my science, (Newtonian mechanical engineer), and all my learning in physics and biology up to that point.

Yet, I knew, more viscerally than anything in my life before, that what I had experienced on the other side of death **was more real than this 3-D, time-space continuum, which we here insist on calling** *reality.* So, I soldiered on, trying to make sense of it all, until I finally connected with others who had also "been there" in the *International Association for Near Death Studies* (IANDS). One of the first things we do with new members at IANDS meetings is to reassure them with, "You are not crazy....you are not alone......we have been there too".

Consequently, if you feel disoriented by what I am saying, just hang on. Shortly, after you adjust your perspective to allow the reality of these facts, then it quickly becomes apparent that,

> *"If we are not actually part of our current carcass, but only occupy it,..... Then it is also reasonable that when our physical carcass is scrapped that our consciousness does not get scrapped with it."*

Instead, it is more reasonable that we (our consciousness) must continue to exist, and very much like we do now. The only changes experienced at *death* are loss of participation in the physical dimensions of 3-D in this space-time reality, but we continue to exist in an alternate reality.

What this means, stated in religious terms is, **"Eternal life is real....**Just as Jesus said.. and also as Plato, the Buddhists and the Egyptians had all said long before Jesus.

PART 1

THE SCIENTIFIC BASIS
and SOME NEGLECTED HISTORY:

CHAPTER 3

NEAR DEATH EXPERIENCES

"If they say to you 'where did you come from?" Say to them, 'We came from The Light".

Jesus, quoted in the Gospel of Thomas,

"In a moment, in the twinkling of an eye.... The dead shall be raised incorruptible and we shall all be changed. "

St. Paul 1 Corinthians 15:51-52
Quoted from the lyrics of Brahm's Requiem (1866/68)

Yes, it really does happen instantaneously, literally *in the twinkling of an eye*. The so-called death is merely a paradigm shift, a complete change of viewpoint. Those left here may call it death while looking at it from this side, but no one ever really dies. What occurs instead is that we merely change our perspective from this habitual frame of reference in 3-D light energy, to a perspective contained in alternative dimensions in dark energy, where the dense hulk of a cadaver is no longer needed and so we simply leave it behind allowing our spirit to expand. Personally, having done that, dying, going out-of-body and then reincarnating back into the same body, has changed everything for me. Here is my personal story.

1970 AD - MY PERSONAL NEAR-DEATH EXPERIENCE: It was in May of 1970, I was in Eugene, Oregon attending college on the G.I. Bill after having served in the Navy during the Vietnam War. I was attending evening classes at the University of Oregon, and working days as a draftsman/engineering technician designing fire sprinkler systems for public buildings. I owned a motorcycle and

MY INTENTION: Personally, I have no axe to grind with those who wish to continue believing the unfounded superstitions with which they have become comfortable. Instead, my desire is only to present the known facts of this alternative paradigm regarding what happens after you die. My intent is to merely provide the information so readers can then choose what they feel most comfortable about believing, instead of being faced only with the choice of blindly accepting or rejecting the superstitions that our western culture has been teaching.

WHAT I KNOW FOR SURE:

From my own Near-Death experience I can confirm that there is much to look forward to after we leave this physical body behind. I am personally convinced that our consciousness moves on to live in a separate dimension. I also know that the afterlife is not a place of retribution or punishment, but that it is merely the next stage of our continuing existence, and that the *life review* which occurs during the death process is not a *final judgment*, as emperor Justinian so hoped he could force all his subjects to believe, but instead serves as the concluding paragraph for the current chapter of our existence.

Consequently, I am not afraid of death.....of course, I do fear the pain of injury, which may occur while I am still left in this physical body, but death itself holds no fear for me because I know as a fact that,

   "DEATH IS NOT FINAL."

I hope, by simply exposing the evidence for consciousness survival which rigorous and replicated science has found to be valid, and making this easily accessible to everyday people, that they too can have the freedom which comes from no longer being afraid of death.

CHAPTER 2

HOW TO USE THIS BOOK

*"The only books that influence us are those for which we
are ready, and which have gone a little further down
our particular path than we have gone ourselves."*
                                   E.M. Forster, Longest Journey, 1907

*"As long as you do not know how to die and come to life
again, You are but a sorry traveler on this dark earth."*
                                   Johann Wolfgang von Goethe

Use this book to prepare for death and as a road map for your
inevitable journey to that "Undiscovered Country".

Part 1 examines the scientific and historical evidence supporting
this new perspective on what death means.

Part 2 is a travel guide to death and the afterlife. It will give you a
detailed account of what death is like, and where we go immediately
thereafter. It talks about what happens as your consciousness continues to exist after you arrive on the other side of the veil in an
alternate dimension, on a higher energy plane.

A New Perspective: Leaving the old view behind
Modern society is often prevented from seeing what rigorous and
replicated science has repeatedly proven to actually be taking
place immediately after the consciousness leaves the physical
body. This cultural perceptive inability is caused primarily by the
following widely held, but mistaken beliefs, all based on comfortable superstitions for which, to date, there is absolutely no evidence:

1. The now obsolete 19ᵗʰ century materialist world view, which categorically denies the existence of anything separate from the physical, including the concept of consciousness or spirit.
2. The western cultures belief in a single lifetime for each soul. This one life perspective was forced upon the entire Roman empire by emperor's Justinian's decree 553 years after Christ. Justinian succeeded in replacing the earlier Christian belief in multiple lifetimes (reincarnation), by hunting down and killing as a heretic anyone who did not subscribe to his single lifetime theory.
3. The widely held religious belief that the entire physical body, and not just the spirit, will be resurrected in any future afterlife. This physical resurrection belief would require consciousness survival to be dependent upon physical survival in a light energy 3-D reality, and rules out the possibility of survival in an alternative dimension existing in dark energy.

Unfortunately, people indoctrinated into the world view created by the above three beliefs do automatically impose these obsolete materialist templates on the death process. Unfortunately, that obscures any real comprehension about what is actually taking place when someone dies.

Consequently, in order to comprehend the alternative paradigm this book offers you, it is essential that you *consciously choose* to alter your perspective of reality and forget the obsolete religion of the science of Newtonian materialism (as still taught in most science curriculums) and instead move into the 21ˢᵗ century understanding of quantum physics. Here is the basis of that altered perspective.

POSTULATE 1: "WE ARE NOT OUR PHYSICAL BODIES, WE ONLY OCCUPY THEM"
It is helpful to use your relation to your car as an illustration. When you drive a car, you use the car very effectively, but during the whole process you are only the *driver* and not actually part of the car. But, the car will respond to your desires fairly accurately and, while some drivers do appear, at least temporarily, to become fused as an actual part of their car, the fact is that they still only "occupy" their car.

Similarly, your relationship to your physical body (carcass) is one of only occupying it temporarily. You are simply "driving" your physical carcass and your body responds to your desires fairly accurately. Using this, "My carcass is like a car" metaphor, let's see how it changes our perspective on life and death.

FIRST CAR FACT: Every few years you buy new tires for your car and throw away the old tires.

SIMILAR CARCASS FACT: Your body does the same thing with cells. It is a long established and carefully verified biological fact that, in a continuous process occurring all the time your body replaces old cells with new ones. In fact, every seven years all the cells in your entire body are replaced with new ones.

The inescapable fact is that today you aren't living in the same physical body cells you were living in eight years ago. No part of your body is the same body it was previously. We make think simplistically that as we get old our body is wearing out, but the truth is that an older person's body is not the same body they occupied when they were younger. It is not even the same body they occupied at middle age. Over each person's lifetime they have slowly moved on to occupy several entirely new carcasses. Suppose that today you are 28 years old then, the fact is, you are now occupying the fourth entirely new body, which has come to you since the one you were born with. All of the cells in your entire body have been replaced at least 4 times and consequently no part of you, not one molecule, is the original physical self.

Now given these facts (which any materialist biologist will verify are true) your consciousness has obviously *transmigrated* (reincarnated) into these replacement cadavers. Four times (if you are now 28 years old) you have moved on into an entirely new body. Just as obviously, the "you" that thinks and feels (your consciousness) is not left behind in those discarded cells. Instead, you merely "inhabit" whatever cells currently are collected together as your physical body. So, your consciousness must then merely occupy your current cadaver like you would occupy your car.

Further, this is nothing new. These are all established biological facts taught in any biology class. So, **it is already proven and well accepted science that you are not those cells that make up your physical body.** But, this truth is conveniently ignored because it is uncomfortable and upsets chosen superstitions.

Actually, if you were, in fact, those original cells and not a separate consciousness (as materialists want to believe), then your consciousness would have disappeared when the first set of cells was replaced with new ones. There would simply have been nothing outside the physical material of the cells to transmigrate. Obviously, that is not what happened, but instead something did transmigrate. Any materialist scientist taking the time to work through this thought experiment will have to finally admit that the only thing we can accurately say with this specific set of facts is that, **"Those discarded cells obviously are not the *real person* and so, despite how uncomfortable it feels, it does appear that you (your consciousness) merely occupies the current group of cells"**.

When we take this one step further it is obvious that the consciousness cannot be part of the physical material of the cadaver's cells, but must then be merely an occupant of those current cells (the current carcass).

SECOND CAR FACT: Every once in a while, when your car's engine or transmission finally wears out, you discard the old engine or transmission and get a new one without replacing the entire car.

SIMILAR CARCASS FACT: Daily, major hospitals perform transplants of entire heart-lung organ systems taken from former living bodies. Skilled surgeons place these "spare parts" into still living bodies and then "restart" those organs. Doing this literally changes out major parts of the original body and the consciousness occupying the repaired body now uses these replacement body parts as their own. So again, it is obvious that if we (our consciousness) were actually part of the cells of the physical body, then that *prior personality* which previously owned and operated those transplanted cells (the donor) ought to arrive along with those transplanted cells. When the organs were then "restarted", the original consciousness of the donor would be vying for control of those organs with the new owner's consciousness.

But, it is obvious from all the times transplants have been successfully preformed that **it is always the consciousness currently occupying the carcass being repaired which now uses those transplanted cells which have been added to their carcass**, and it is not the consciousness of the donor who used those cells previously who continues with those cells.

Again this undeniably demonstrates that the still living consciousness which was previously using this carcass before their old heart-lung cells were removed, has *transmigrated* (reincarnated) into the transplanted organs and cells. There is also no part of that deceased donor's consciousness, which previously occupied the heart-lung cells still present. Instead, the heart-lung cells have a new driver.

Obviously, from these facts both the consciousness now operating the reused heart-lung system, and the prior owner/operator of those organs only "occupy" the cells, and neither the prior owner's nor the new owner's consciousness is in any way "inherent" in the physical material itself. So then it is only obvious that each consciousness must be just a passenger in the body and not part of the physical material of the carcass itself.

BRAIN TRANSPLANTS: In the near future some doctor will figure out how to perform a brain transplant. When this happens the transplanted brain will follow the same principles as the transplanted heart. The consciousness that occupies that transplanted brain will be the still living personality whose cadaver received the transplant and will not be the prior consciousness that previously occupied that donated brain.

This should be the *coup de grace* for the outdated 19th century idea that "mind" is a mere outgrowth of the wet brain. When a completely different mind is using the same wet brain that was previously occupied by a prior mind, it will show that the brain is just a tool (a servo-mechanism like a foot or a hand) and that the physical cells are not the source of the consciousness. The first brain transplant will clearly show that the consciousness is no derivative byproduct of the wet brain, but is instead a separate entity that merely occupies it, and that the wet brain is the derivative by-product of the mind which pre-existed it. At this point materialist biologists will no longer be able to deny transmigration (reincarnation) as a fact.

TRACE PERSONALITY TRAITS DO TRANSPLANT: An interesting aside, which I intend to fully discuss in a future book, is the now well documented fact that some of the "feelings" (emotional attachments) associated with the personality which previously occupied the heart-lung being transplanted do indeed make the transition. For example, a middle aged woman who had never liked beer, green peppers or chicken nuggets, received a heart-lung transplant from an anonymous donor. Later, while still in recovery from the operation, she began to wildly crave beer, chicken nuggets and green peppers. She wrote a book[2] detailing her investigation in which she tracked down the donor, only to find that he was a

Hossack's interest in physics is in keeping with his position as a professor in his former physical lifetime. And so it appears that Hossack got together with other like-minded survivors on the other side and studied these things there. Much of what he related involved quantum mathematics which was not known when Dr. Hossack himself was alive, and also was not known when Randall wrote about the conversation in 1906, but would be discovered 40 years later.

> **Note:** My further research on Dr. Hassock has found that he graduated from Princeton University and received his medical degree in Philadelphia in 1791, and subsequently studied abroad at Edinburgh, Scotland before returning to New York. Dr. Hossack was one of the founders of the New York Historical Society in 1804, and also established the Elgin Botanical Garden between 47th and 51st Streets and between 5th and 6th (Avenue of the Americas) in Manhattan.

WHAT IS THE AFTERLIFE LIKE: Randall went further and asked several disincarnate spirits about what the afterlife is like:

> *"The so called dead live here about us.... The substance that forms the bodies of spirit-people, vibrating at more than five octaves higher than the violet-ray* (violet = 7.5 x 10^{14}hz, double that 5 times), *few in earth life ever see, though spirit-people see and talk with each other and with mortals when the necessary conditions are secured.....I know that every hope, ambition, and desire of earth are continued beyond this life, as is also the burden of wrong (karma). I know that we are as much a spirit now as we ever shall be, that in death, so called, we simply vacate and discard this gross material that gives us expression in the physical plane."*[56]

> Edward C. Randall

Randall's description of beings in the afterlife living right around us but at a higher vibration coincides with quantum field theory (string theory) which postulates 8 additional hidden energy fields (M-theory) which exist "around us" but have not yet been discerned.

Randall's reports of what the people on the other side told him, are strikingly similar to what the "Masters" are reported to have told Dr. Brian Weiss nearly a hundred years later. Randall's reports also agree with what the Near-Death people have been reporting in the 21st century about how the "veil is lifted" and reality is glimpsed. Also, in each of these separate cases, when the consciousness is leaving the physical dimension and going to an alternative reality they all report hearing a noise which sounds like a rushing wind.

As a student of physics, I speculate that this rushing wind sound is caused by the speeding up of their vibrations to suit the higher frequencies of the new plane of reality to which they are going, for example:

1. Thoth-Hermes in 2500 BC described these alternative realities as seven planes with many levels in each plane. He also said everything was made of vibrations (string theory).
2. The "masters" told Dr. Weiss that there are seven planes with many levels.
3. A surviving consciousness from the other side told Edward C. Randall that

> "There are innumerable spheres in the spirit world if it were not so progression would be a myth....some tell you that there are only seven. That is because they have no knowledge beyond that sphere (seven). I do not mean a place fixed by boundaries for the spheres or degrees in spirit life are only conditions and are not confined to a limited space....As a soul develops it naturally arises above its surroundings, and consequently experiences a change in its spheres or conditions (chakras)."

DARK ENERGY: Just what are these alternate dimensions where these surviving consciousness exist, and which apparently surrounds us? The Quantum Mechanics of the late 20th century points to the fact that the universe is not made of empty space, as we like to imagine it, but that instead all of space is filled with dark energy. An energy force which we can prove by using quantum mathematics must be there, but which we have not yet been able to discern. What this energy might be we cannot yet measure with our crude instruments of measurement. Yet, back in 1906, before Einstein's theory was published, Edward C. Randal had this to say after he held ADC discussions with Michael Faraday, Denton, and Dr. Hossack:

> "*They believe the spiritual plane is filled with aether* (dark matter) *similar to earth substance* (light matter) *but in a very high state of vibration...... According to them, the universe is all material substance or matter in different and varying states of vibration.*"[57]
>
> Edward C. Randall

Indeed, this is a statement of the alternative dimensions postulated by String Theory. Further, Dr. Hossack in another after death communication told Randall that:

> "*The most learned scientist among the inhabitants of earth has practically no conception of the properties of matter, the substance of the universe, the visible and the invisible. I did not when I lived among you though I made a special study of the subject. That, which you see and touch making up the physical or tangible, and having three dimensions (3D), is the lowest or crudest expression of life force and not withstanding my long study of the subject, the idea that the physical (matter) had a permanent life form or that what you call space*

was composed of matter filled with intelligent and comprehensive life
(conscious universe) *in a higher vibration* (separate energy field)
*never occurred to me. So when I became an in habitant of the plane
where I now reside, I was wholly unprepared to grasp or comprehend
the material conditions of the environment in which I found
myself.*"[58,59]

The subject under discussion is clearly the Zero Point Energy field
and dark energy which would not be discovered until many decades
later...... Now, whether Randall was actually speaking with Dr. Hossack, Faraday and Denton is up to you to decide..... But, Randall, a
New York lawyer and not a physicist is obviously reporting something which is completely unknown to 19th century materialist science in his time, and which we only began to discover nearly half a
century later, but which those same gentlemen claiming to be
speaking to him would have understood completely when they were
living in a fourth dimension energy field called the afterlife. This
brings us now to the subject of quantum energy fields which will be
discussed in the following chapter.

CHAPTER 6

CONSCIOUSNESS & QUANTUM FIELD THEORY

"When you can measure what you are speaking about, and express it in numbers, you know something about it; But when you cannot measure it, when you cannot express it in numbers, your knowledge is of a meager and unsatisfactory kind; It may be the beginning of knowledge, but you have scarcely in your thoughts advanced to the state of Science, *whatever the matter may be."*

Lord Kelvin (Sir William Thomson), PLA, vol. 1, "Electrical
Units of Measurement",1883-05-03

"There is no place in this new kind of Physics (Quantum Mechanics) for the field and (also) matter, for the field is the only reality"

Albert Einstein

"How often has "Science" killed off all spook philosophy, laid ghosts and raps and "telepathy" away underground as so much popular delusion", and yet, "The phenomena are there.....lying broadcast over the surface of history."

William James

"As far as Myers could see, traditional science and religion seemed interested only in proving themselves, not in resolving confusion".

Deborah Blum (P. 49 *Ghost Hunters* © 2006)

> *"Physics has become a branch of psychology.... Physics is the study of the structure of the consciousness."*
> Gary Zukav, *The Dancing Wu Li Masters: An Overview of the New Physics* ©1979, p. 31 Bantam 1980 edition

One of the first objections usually raised against the existence of the afterlife is, "Well, O.K. I will admit that there is a great deal of evidence, but where could the afterlife possibly exist?" The short answer is in the dark energy of the conscious universe.

NEW SCIENCE:

Today, there is a revolution taking place in subatomic particle physics, which is altering our world view and replacing it with an entirely new ontology. This revolution is similar to the one which took place when Newtonian physics toppled the church's world view in the 18th and 19th centuries, and unfortunately it is faced with just as much skepticism from the old guard.

This new paradigm includes a *conscious universe*. Many physicists now believe that the underlying building block of all reality is, in fact, consciousness (mind). In other words, the Universe itself thinks. This is a whole new area of the physics of Quantum Mind, which inserts consciousness into the Schrodinger and Dirac equations to bring about the state vector collapse, as discussed below.

Yet, this is exactly the same theory that Dr. Hossack (quoted in the previous chapter) was saying back in 1906, while speaking from the other side as a surviving consciousness. He pre-shadowed our 21st century concept of a *conscious universe* when he stated,
> *"the idea that the physical (matter) had a permanent life form or that what you call space was composed of matter filled with intelligent and comprehensive life* (existing there) *in a higher vibration* (separate energy field) *never occurred to me* (when he was living here in the physical reality of light energy)."

The current paradigm shift in physics began 80 years ago with the start of quantum mechanics and the later discoveries built on that understanding, which now show that those energy fields which manifest for us in 3-D, and which we perceive as being the extent of our material reality, are actually empowered with light energy which makes up only 4% of the energy in the universe. That light energy

Alan Hugenot

materializes spontaneously from dark energy which is held in another undiscerned dimension, but which makes up the other 96% of the energy of the universe. Following is the story of the discovery of dark energy and what it means in relation to consciousness survival.

ZERO POINT FIELDS (Dark Energy):

Back in the 19th century the majority of materialist scientists believed that what we now call *space,* was not empty but was filled with a substance they called the aether. Nikola Testla believed it was filled with energy.

> *"We are whirling through endless space, with an inconceivable speed, all around us everything is spinning, everything is moving, everywhere there is energy... There must be some way of availing ourselves of this energy more directly. Then, with the light obtained from the medium, with the power derived from it, with every form of energy obtained without effort, from the store forever inexhaustible, humanity will advance with giant strides. The mere contemplation of these magnificent possibilities expands our minds, strengthens our hopes and fills our hearts with supreme delight."*
>
> *Nikola Tesla, referring to Zero Point Energy in 1891*

But, later the results of the Michelson/Morley experiment banished the concept of an aether from our early twentieth century physics.

Unfortunately, this 20th century aether-less interpretation left a hole (pardon the pun) in our explanation of the universe. If there were no aether filling space then it seemed that interstellar space had nothing within it which could allow the propagation of electro-magnetic waves (EMF). So, with no energy to support the energy transfer how could the radio waves or light waves from distant stars ever reach us?

On the other hand, classical Newtonian physics had also predicted that when a substance is lowered to the temperature of absolute zero, -273°C (-459.67°F), all energetic behavior should theoretically cease. Yet, it was discovered (through many replicated experiments) that when elementary particles were lowered to this "zero point" that such activity did not cease and the particles continued to exhibit energetic behavior.

This conundrum continued until physicists discovered mathematically, that what we perceive as the vacuum of interstellar space cannot possibly be empty, but must actually be filled with this undetected energy fields of dark energy (dimensions 4-D through

11-D). And, that undetected energy is the substance which actually holds matter (our physical perception) together. Indeed, the mathematics works out to show that the light energy which we can perceive in our 3-D physical mindset, actually represents only about 4% of the total energy that is known to exist in interstellar space. This means that the other 96% of the energy which we have not yet been able to perceive is made up of un-discernable dark energy and dark matter which is collectively described as the Zero Point Field or just "dark energy".[60] At this date we don't know where this energy comes from nor how it is transformed from dark energy to light energy. Yet, without the instantaneous and continuous conversion of energy from that ZPF into our 3-D light energy, which occurs all the time and sustains our perceived reality (our 3-D universe as we know it) would instantly cease to exist. Like a plasma HD flat screen that loses its power, we and all of what we call the physical world, would become a fading blip (a dying singularity).

> *"There is a dynamic equilibrium in which the zero-point energy stabilizes the electron in a set ground-state orbit. It seems that the very stability of matter itself appears to depend on an underlying sea of electromagnetic zero-point energy."*
> The New Scientist July 1987

The honest truth is that we don't yet discern 96% (dark energy) of what is happening around us all the time. It as if we are blind folded by out Newtonian materialist mindset, but foolishly insist on believing we can see everything clearly in the meager 4% (light energy) which we can actually detect. So, how can we assume to know all there is to know from the small portion we can discern?

This Zero-Point field is an undetected mass of potential and un-manifest energy where particles and antiparticles spontaneously arise and then disappear, and of which we know next to zero.

If you want to know the background behind all this new exciting physics I invite you to read the references on subatomic theory listed in the end notes, but keep in mind the findings of the *Copenhagen Interpretation* of quantum mechanics (1927). An "interpretation" which is a rough agreement between Neils Bohr, Werner Heisenberg, and others including Max Born, which explains their vision of quantum mechanics:

> *"A complete understanding of reality lies beyond the capabilities of rational thought".*[61] Copenhagen Interpretation of Quantum Mechanics (1927)

Loosely translated this means that, "*whether or not something is true is never a matter of how closely it corresponds to the absolute truth, but is instead a matter of how consistent it happens to be with our own personal perceptions and experience.*"A famous physicist Richard Feynman said it more succinctly,

> "*I think I can safely say that nobody understands Quantum Mechanics*"

> Richard Feynman (theoretical physicist 1918-1988)

STRING THEORY & UNDISCERNED DIMENSIONS: Underlying the discovery of dark matter and multiple undiscerned dimensions is *String Theory*. Simply stated, string theory suggests that the smallest *particles* or fundamental constituents of reality are not point-like particles (such as the concepts we have for protons, neutrons and electrons), but are instead similar to tiny strings vibrating at different frequencies, but without any string actually being there, and only a vibration. The ancient Egyptian Thoth-Hermes correlated this theory when he stated back in 2500BC that, "The universe is made of vibrations".

This string theory can be used to successfully show linkages between gravity and the other fundamental forces in physics. However, these linkages only work if there are 10 or more dimensions instead of the 3 we can currently discern.

M-THEORY: Unfortunately, string theorists discovered that five different strains of string theory which concisely explain how the universe works also come from five seemingly irreconcilable perspectives. But, they also discovered that when you added an *eleventh dimension* then everything makes sense. This eleven dimension theory is known as M-theory.

Never-the-less, these non-detectable energy fields, which mathematically "must" exist, do provide a suitable location for the afterlife to exist and where the surviving consciousness can be postulated to be hanging out. Indeed, we can further postulate that un-discerned dark energy forms several unseen energy fields around us all the time. So if you feel the presence of a departed loved one's soul, you may not be merely superstitious, but are actually feeling them there in the ZPF surrounding you.

> "*According to quantum field theory, fields alone are real. They are the substance of the universe and not "matter"* ....*Matter (particles) is simply the momentary manifestations of interacting fields which, intangible and insubstantial as they are, are the only real things in the universe* ....

"According to Buddhist theory, reality is "virtual" in nature. What appear to be "real" objects in it, like trees and people, actually are transient illusions which result from a limited mode of awareness.................. The illusion is that parts of an overall virtual process are "real" (permanent) "things".................

"Enlightenment" is the experience that "things" including "I" are transient, virtual states devoid of separate existences, momentary links between illusions of the past and illusions of the future unfolding in the illusion of time".

Gary Zukav, The Dancing Wu Li Masters: An Overview of the New Physics
©1979, p. 200...p.236 Bantam 1980 edition

From the above three quotes it is apparent that ancient Buddhist teaching from 2500+ years ago, simply mirrors quantum field theory of the 20th and 21st century. Buddhist teaching philosophically explains the same phenomenon that quantum field theory explains mathematically.

Also, since the early 20th century quantum field theory has conceived the axiom that.

"Fields, and the interaction of fields, is all that really exists".

THE LAW OF CONSCIOUS UNIVERSE:[62] In ancient Egypt Thoth-Hermes said, "The Universe is mental". Literally, this translates to "The Universe is made of thoughts". Quantum mechanics has recently shown that we live in a *conscious universe* and that the basic building block of everything in this universe is consciousness (thoughts). Quantum mechanics has recently given us two principles which show "the universe is mental", these are known as *non-locality* and the *uncertainty principle*.

"The undeniable existence of human consciousness set against the absence of any satisfactory scientific account for it.......
suggests to me that something is seriously amiss with the contemporary Western scientific worldview. For a long time I could not put my finger on exactly what it was. Then, about four years ago, I suddenly realized where the error lies.

Rather than assuming that consciousness somehow arises from the material world, as most scientists do,..........we need to consider the alternative worldview put forward by many metaphysical and spiritual traditions...... in which consciousness is held to be a fundamental component of reality. As fundamental as space, time, and matter,...... perhaps even more so....... When we do, everything changes, and everything remains the same." [63]

Peter Russell *2001*

NON LOCALITY: Since the 1930's physicists have observed a subtle kind of information transfer, which is also called the Einstein, Podolsky, Rosen (EPR) correlation, or "entanglement". It was first discussed in a famous paper (1930) by Albert Einstein, Boris Podolsky, and Nathan Rosen. Experiments on photons and other particles have repeatedly confirmed these "entanglement" correlations, thereby providing strong evidence for the ultimate validity of quantum mechanics. Particle physicists now know that two "related" subatomic particles, no matter how widely separated, even by a distance of thousands of light years, are not actually separate (i.e. non-local while they appear to be dimensionally widely separated, they are in fact in the same locality). If you think long enough about that you are eventually forced to come to the realization that space is an illusion. An easier way to express it is that,

> *"The particles themselves don't have a specific location, but exist simultaneously in multiple localities."*

That's right, they appear to be in more than one place at the same time.

The EPR Correlation, known to physicists as "non-locality", has now been shown to exist and has been replicated in four historic experiments,[64] John S. Bell, a physicist at CERN the European Organization for Nuclear Research located in Switzerland, in 1964 published a mathematical "proof" for entanglement (non-locality), which he hoped to disprove, but which has since become known as Bell's Theorem. The Theorem was polished and re-worked over the following decade until it arrived in its present form. The mathematics are indecipherable to non-mathematicians, but it's implications profoundly affect our basic world view. **Many physicists today believe that Bell's Theorem is the most important single work in the history of physics**. Bell's Theorem tells us clearly that there is no such thing as a separate part (the space between things or the separation.... is completely an illusion).

> *"All parts of the Universe are connected in an intimate and immediate way".*

This, at least so far, allows only one rational explanation, which is that the universe itself is conscious (intelligent). Basically, Bell's Theorem and the enlightened metaphysical experience of *unity* are compatible. The theorem is a mathematical proof that,

> *"If the statistical predictions of quantum theory are correct, then some of our commonsense ideas about the world are profoundly mistaken".*

HISTORY OF BELLE'S THEOREM: In 1964 Bell's Theorem was an untested theory the correlations had been calculated, but not tested. However, in 1972 John Clauser and Stuart Freedman at Lawrence Berkeley Laboratory performed an experiment to confirm or disprove the predicted correlations. They found that the statistical predictions upon which Bell's Theorem is based are indeed correct.

Then in 1982, Alan Aspect, a physicist at the Institute of Optics, University of Paris, in Orsay, France, replicated the Clauser-Freedman experiments while also improving the apparatus so that it could now be changed micro-seconds before the measurement was taken, (i.e. this way the experiment apparatus did not allow sufficient time for information to travel from point A to point B at the speed of light), and yet the effect of the change was already *known* to the previously entangled particle at point B, instantaneously and long before any signal (traveling at the speed of light) could have possibly reached it from the other entangled particle at point A.

This was replicated yet a third time in experiments carried out in 1996 at University of Geneva by W. Tittel* and his team (J. Brendel, B., T. Herzog, H. Zbinden, and N. Gisin) which duplicated Alan Aspects apparatus and found the same results, and was published in July 1997. These results were replicated a fourth time in August 1998 by Gregor Weihs and his team at University of Innsbruck.

WHAT REPLICATION MEANS: In scientific inquiry, whenever you can replicate a predicted result, it amounts to an unassailable truth. So, the only explanation for these observed and replicated phenomena is that the two widely separated yet entangled particles are not actually separated, ... but are rather in intimate contact. (i.e. They are both in exactly the same location even though they are perceived as being in widely separated locations). This is called *non-locality*, or the non-reality of the concept of location. In other words, as the Buddhist thought teaches, **"What we think we observe as space is just an illusion".** Here is what one prominent physicist believes about all this:

> "*Everything we know about Nature is in accord with the idea that the fundamental process of Nature lies outside space and time........ But generates events that can be located in space-time*".

> "*Bell's theory (non-locality) shows that our ordinary ideas about the world are somehow profoundly deficient even on the macroscopic level*",
> Henry P. Stapp quantum physicist U. Cal.

UNCERTAINITY PRINCIPLE: The second principle which postulates a conscious universe is Heisenberg's "Principle of Uncertainty" (also called complementarity). This can most easily be understood in the fact that light exhibits two separate ways of being. Sometimes it will act like a particle, other times it acts like a wave. But, most interestingly,

"which one it will become (a wave or a particle) responds to what the researcher conducting the experiment is looking for".

When the scientist is experimenting to prove that it is a wave, the light acts like a wave, his consciousness causes the state vector collapse. This is known as the *Measurement Problem.* If the scientist is trying to prove that it is a particle, then the light acts like a particle. The light actually allows the scientist to choose how it will be. This phenomena with light has been replicated dozens of times.

This means that in this conscious universe, you (the experimenter) are participating in the outcome of the experiment. Another way to say it is that your consciousness is affecting the conscious universe supporting the experiment itself.

The dimensions used to measure classical reality (length, width, depth) are actually just ideas or concepts we choose to use in envisioning our reality. Everything is made of sub-atomic particles, and sub-atomic particles are merely correlations, created when two energy fields interact. In other words if we weren't here to envision (think up) the correlations, then there would not be any correlations and therefore no waves or particles" (i.e. no state vector collapse), or more bluntly,

"Everything is made of thoughts held in the universe's consciousness and projected on the veil of reality.

6000 or more years ago Thoth-Hermes told the ancient Egyptians, "Everything is made of vibrations (waves)". And, "the Universe is mental".

Today, this is where quantum mechanics has also arrived. So it is no surprise that suddenly particle physicists are all busily trying to explain that the Universe itself is one big inseparable consciousness, and that we are all part of the whole (unity). But, the ancient sage Thoth-Hermes clearly had already said this same thing thousands of years earlier.

All of which brings us back to quantum field theory mentioned earlier in the chapter. Quantum field theory is based on the assumption that *physical reality is essentially non-substantial.* Fields alone are real. Fields are the substance of the universe and not *matter.* Matter or particles are simply instantaneous manifestations of interacting fields. Everything that we think is real is just a perception of those fields.

"We perceive it..... therefore it is."
(consciousness dictates the state vector collapse)

Sounds a lot like mind over matter, and yet, that is exactly what it is. According to quantum mechanics, and Thoth-Hermes mind over matter is precisely how the universe operates.

THE MEASUREMENT PROBLEM: The concepts of our Newtonian materialist physics, which are based on the Cartesian objective perspective, force us into the idea that we can observe something objectively (from outside itself) by simply separating ourselves from the experiment and then observing what happens from an unbiased position totally outside the box.

But, because the universe is non-local it is not possible to be *outside of the box,* and we actually can not separate ourselves out of the whole in order to actually make an impartial and objective measurement. We and our consciousness are always involved in the state vector collapse which causes reality. This is the measurement problem the fact that consciousness itself is causal to our perceived reality. It is an especially difficult problem for materialists who do not want to admit the idea that consciousness could exist prior to or without matter existing first. Yet, consciousness is what precipitates matter out of infinite potentiality.

Instead of a fixed state, reality exists as an infinite number of potentialities (as expressed by the Schrodinger or Dirac equations) and only one of those potentialities will be precipitated in order to be measured. The conscious will of the observer provides the choice of which one of the potentialities will be observed. This *choice* is known as the state vector collapse, and it is caused by the hidden variables of conscious will inserted as a factor into the equations mentioned.

MIND OVER MATTER: Proof of the action of these hidden variables can be found in the work of *Princeton Engineering Anomalies Research* (PEAR) laboratory, which was founded in 1979, and has been continuously studying *the role of consciousness in the establishment of reality.* At PEAR some 50 million experimental trials have been performed, containing more than three billion bits of binary information.....Anomalous correlations of the machine outputs with pre-stated operator intentions are clearly evident.... and statistically replicable. Over the total data base, composite anomaly is unlikely by chance to about one part per one billion. In laymen's terms this means:

"After 30 years of continual testing PEAR has overwhelmingly shown that mind influences matter every time and with odds better than a billion to one."

In other words using double blind studies PEAR has consistently shown that mental effort can control machines.

Using people off the street who volunteer to come in with no preparation or practice to try to influence the outcome of machines, PEAR watches these novices tilt the odds in their favor every time, simply re-proving Heisenberg's uncertainty principle (complementarity) over and over again.

"Ordinary people have the capacity to alter what machines do" (by mental effort alone)[65]

Elizabeth Lloyd Mayer, Ph.D.

THE PHYSICS OF CONSCIOUSNESS: For decades neuroscientists, psychologists, and brain researchers have been struggling to explain the phenomena of consciousness. Recently Evan Walker Ph.D. in Physics, and founder of the Walker Cancer Institute has postulated a clear path to explaining consciousness through quantum physics. In his book *The Physics of Consciousness* ©2000[66] he explains how the operation of bizarre properties of elementary particles support a new theory of reality, based on the principles of quantum physics. His theory answers such questions as "What is the nature of consciousness?", "What is the nature of will?", "What is the source of material reality?"

TOWARD A SOLUTION TO THE MEASUREMENT PROBLEM: Walker resolves consciousness and inserts it into the Schrodinger equation as a "hidden variable", following concepts conceived by David Bohm, and explains how the conscious will actually collapses the state vector into one state out of the myriad potentialities available according to Schrodinger's equation. He examines this in the light of Ehrenfest's Theorem showing how Schrodinger's equation causes objects in the macroscopic world to obey the laws of classical physics, and the exceptions to Ehrenfest's Theorem. He shows how quantum mechanical state selection is non-local, and how the will selects the state of the brain that we consciously experience, and also how at the same time the global nature of quantum mechanics of necessity then links this brain state to the external events that occur. He coordinates consciousness and the state vector collapse to solve the Einstein-Podolsky-Rosen (EPR) paradox in rigid conformity to the Lorentz invariance.[67]

He then exposes our problems with understanding these phenomena which are deeply entwined with the fact that our consciousness is filled with such vast amounts of "noise" that the will often cannot decipher what is the predominate desire.

The will channel carries the "signal" that selects events by means of state vector collapse, but the consciousness channel is only so much noise by comparison. The signal to noise ratio of the mind is simply a very small number. This is conundrum is both what causes positive intention (or prayer) to work, and also what makes it seemingly so difficult to control.

The basic hypothesis underlying all of Walker's theorem is that, "All observers share a fragment of their mind experience, non-locally and non-temporally (i.e. outside space and time), and this is forced on us by the underlying physics." Consequently, since we mutually share some of the consciousness channel, the signal to noise ratio is further perturbed, making state vector collapse prediction even more difficult.

Walker's elegant resolution, which removes much of the uncertainty of the Copenhagen interpretation, is a wonderful read for anyone who understands the basics of sub-atomic particle theory, and understanding his postulates goes a long way in explaining how quantum physics supports the existence of an afterlife in an alternative dimension outside space and time. So, I recommend taking the time to fully understand his postulates.

Walker firmly establishes consciousness as an integral element of quantum mechanics. He shows what the physical side of "observation" is all about, and his solution is at the heart of *the measurement problem* in quantum physics. He shows the two sides of reality that cause the state vector collapse and bring about consciousness as an integral part of the physical world. His presentation is a tour d' force of *the measurement problem*, but leaves you with the realization that we can not use reductionist thinking to comprehend this by attempting to analyze one element at a time. Instead we will have to examine and see, all at once, how they fit together. Walker shows the nature of what reality becomes when all the prior work on consciousness and *the measurement problem* are extended to round everything out, and that "all at once" is what a mountain top experience (the "aha" moment) is all about. Finally, Walker elegantly ties consciousness into Dirac's equation which ultimately resolves into the understanding that,

> "There is no space, as such, no matter, as such, there exists only the observer consciously experiencing his or her compliment, and in doing so, the "observer" weaves the illusion of space-time and matter falls like snow from the conscious loops of the mind." [68]

THE QUANTUM HOLOGRAM

The recent invention of *functional Magnetic Resonance Imaging* (fMRI) brings all this theory together in a practical example. fMRI has shown us that an entire blueprint for our body is contained as a holographic image embedded in every part of any organism of that body. By setting up an apparatus that detects the p-car of magnetic energy which originates within that isolated part so we can re-create a holographic representation of the entire blueprint for the organism.

This fMRI phenomenon also provides proof of a massive information storage server, a data base which fills the entire universe (literally an Akashic record). Everything which we perceive here, all the substance of the earth, provides itself as a gigantic information storage device.

On the other hand, fMRI shows that this same information, which it now allows us to detect, has always been there undetected since the beginning of history. Unfortunately, this Akashic record, although surmised by the ancients, lay just beyond the perceptive framework our 19th century concepts of Newtonian physics. In fact, it was those chosen constrictions on our vision, our Cartesian frame of reference, that simply "ruled it out" of our reality. But, having discovered that it was always there it becomes obvious that there is probably a great deal more that our classical materialist world view does not yet include within its narrow definitions of objective reality and which we therefore have not yet discerned.

QUANTUM HOLOGRAPHY: The concept of a holographically-based information storage system in the Universe (literally stored everywhere) was originally argued by physicist David Bohm and Karl Pribram,[69] a neurophysiologist from Stanford University. They postulated the evidence suggests that our world and everything in it, are just projections from a level of reality so beyond our own dimensions of 3-D that it is outside both space and time. And, like Sheldrake's Morphic Fields Bohm & Pribram found that Holographs have a property called *distributedness*, where any fractional portion of the hologram contains sufficient information to reconstruct the complete original 3-D information pattern.

Since every system is loosely coupled with the energetic state of its surroundings, information from a system is stored in the surrounding environment through a process of decoherence in which. entanglements are generated between the system and environment. This has the effect of sharing quantum information with—or transferring it to—the surroundings. This might be compared with how a heated object will give off its heat to the surrounding colder environment. This heat loss is irreversible, and likewise so is the decoherence information transfer irreversible, and is therefore a permanent record.

For more on this see Henry P. Stapp's 2007 text on Mindful Universe[70] Stapp is a theoretical physicist at the University of California's Lawrence Berkeley Laboratory.

But, if such a storage system as this, which is equivalent to the Akashic Record spoken of in the Hindu text *Samkhya Karika* (circa 200 AD), can exist *everywhere* in the universe, then how are these universal information storage servers accessed, read and interpreted?. How do remote viewing clairvoyants and mediums tap into this record? To understand how such undetected energy could exist in a totally undetected state, the effects of which are only occasionally observed, let's consider the science of holographic projections.

UNDERSTANDING HOLOGRAPHIC PROJECTION: Holographic projections are a light projection phenomena which illustrates how retrieval of information in an Akashic field might actually work. If you have ever been to see a holographic projection in 3-D, you may already know that it is achieved by the projection of two invisible fields or planes of light. They are projected in such a coordinated way that wherever the planes intersect (and therefore react) there is a visual effect created that appears to be very real, and actually visible in high definition 3-D. Yet, the projection is no more than a technologically achieved apparition.

PHASE CONJUGATION (P-CAR): In order to become visible in our three dimensional space time context, a holographic information transmission requires two optical waves known as the reference wave and the object wave. When these two waves interfere they make a 3-D holographic image in space-time. Both waves are spatially and temporally coherent at the moment of creation, and are then separated to travel different paths.

The object wave is directed towards the object where it experiences intensity changes and phase-shifts. In a normal 2-D photograph we optically record only the intensity changes of the object wave and not the phase-shifts. But, when a reference wave is also directed back towards the emitted object wave, then an interference pattern is created.

This interference pattern also records the phase-shifts of the object wave relative to the reference wave. It is these phase-shifts that then produce the perception in space-time of the 3-D image.

To make this more understandable, think of the blue and red sun glasses you might wear in a 3-D movie. This adjusts your eyes to a phase shift. Or, you may have viewed old photos in s stero-optical viewer.

In the animal kingdom, dolphins, bats, fish, flies, birds, and yes, even humans all process their sensory information holographically. Dolphins and bats actually create holograms by transmitting acoustic reference and object waves (P-car) that are then reflected back to the mammal for neural processing. Studies in humans have shown that the holographic concept exists not only on the neural level, but also on the cellular and molecular levels.

EMOTIONAL P-CAR: Now, going a step further, but still using the holographic projection as an example. If we can simply imagine consciousness as *mental projection* and the emotional as *soul or heart projection* being two similar, but separate, projections of non-detectable dark energy fields (similar to a light energy holographic projection). It becomes easy to see that when these two dark energy fields intersect with each other they will become detectable due to Phase Conjugation (p-car).

As early as 1948, Jan Ehrenwald, M.D. proposed a similar theory for ESP in *Telepathy and Medical Psychology*[71] including a telepathic P-car which he called "scatter effect" to describe the fact that telepathic communications often tend to be fragmented and scattered both spatially and temporally (Walker describes this as *noise*). Ehrenwald regarded telepathy as a "bi-phasic" involving at first a "cataphysic" phase (or fragmentation effect separating the two signals), followed by a an anaphysic phase where a picture comes together in an accurate presentation, or to use Walker's terminology we could call the mental projection the *consciousness channel* and the emotional projection the *will channel*.

If we extend this line of thinking, the undetectable surviving consciousness of deceased individuals which sometimes appear, under proper circumstances, as apparitions, now become easily feasible as being mental projections (telepathic) rather than actual "sightings" of the individual.

The survival of the consciousness stored in such an undetectable energy field also seems easily possible. Indeed, just as possible as Marconi's "invisible" radio waves. Today, one hundred years after Marconi most of us now believe in radio, television and cell phones because we see the effects all the time. But, the electro magnetic field (EMF) or radio waves were always there long before they were discovered. The energy which provides the propagation for cell phones was lying there unused 100,000 years ago when ignorant cavemen were eating flesh from mastodon bones. Those radio waves were not invented by Lodge and Marconi, but merely discovered by them and put to use. Yet, at the end of the 19th century and in the early 20th, even after Marconi had proved his wireless many leading scientists thought, "Marconi was a phony".

Today, with regard to the afterlife, we are like those cavemen.... very ignorant of the non-discernible dark energy fields which currently surround us.

EVIDENCE OF MACRO-SCALE QUANTUM HOLOGRAMS & INFORMATION STORAGE: The fact that the universe indeed stores massive amounts of information was discovered in the 1950's when George DelaWarr, built a remote imaging camera which uses a small DNA sample to photographically image the subject's internal conditions at a distance, with a high degree of accuracy and was able to detect diseases in pre-clinical stages. Using a small piece of

DNA DelaWarr could "image" the entire body it came from, and diagnose its existing diseases. Theoretically this system is detecting and recording quantum holographic information.[72]

The smallest DNA sample apparently carries complete information about the entire subject body from which it was taken, carried as a complete quantum hologram that can affect optical systems and, under the right conditions, produce a holographic-like image.

A MECHANISM FOR REMOTE VIEWING, SECOND SIGHT & APPARITIONS: When there is no EMF signal present to create p-car conditions to allow normal decoding of the quantum hologram, apparently there are other as yet undetected transmission mechanisms in addition to EMF (i.e. dark energy). Apparently, all that is required to tap into these undetected mechanisms is to allow the brain of a sensitive person (medium) to focus on an object and to establish a resonant relationship, which then enhances formation of the p-car coherence, that allows the information to be accurately perceived, even at great distances. Although this transmission mechanism is as yet undetermined, it is obvious that many sensitives (mediums) use it.

Further, since any waves reverberating through the universe will remain coherent with the waves at the source they are sufficient to serve as the reference to decode the holographic information of any quantum hologram emanating from remote locations (Marcer 1998).[73] But, are there such subtle, as yet undiscovered, transmission systems?

DNA OPTICAL RADIATION: Russian scientists have recently measured a subtle holographic bioenergy radiation that is linked to physical DNA. This subtle energy system appears to be an intact energy field containing relevant organismal information that is capable of being coupled to an optical imaging device.[74,75,] And, for this system to work, the observer which is sensing the information, and the recorded source of information must be in a resonant relationship for the information to be accurately perceived (i.e. must have established p-car or quantum resonance).

This non-local, quantum hologram is the first mechanism which is fully compatible with quantum mechanics and also works with the macro-scale three dimensional world which we know as 3-D reality. Further, it also allows us many possible solutions in the field of consciousness research. *Functional Magnetic Resonance Imaging* (fMRI),

(Schempp 1992), which validated the recovery and utilization of non-local quantum information using quantum holography. Also, Marcer (1995), Hammeroff (1994) and Penrose have presented further data supporting additional quantum processes.[76]

REMOTE VIEWING – the science supporting it:

This brings us to Remote Viewing. Hal Puthoff and Russell Targ spent many years at Stanford Research Institute (SRI) researching the phenomena of remote viewing on secret projects funded by the U.S. Federal government.[77] They measured and documented remote viewing using double blind studies to determine whether this phenomenon actually existed. Targ calls these the Remote Viewing Projects and has written several books on this demonstrating the statistical success they had which prove that Clairvoyance (remote viewing) as a human power is valid.

Elisabeth Mayer[78] also described this remote viewing work in great detail including interviews with Harold Puthoff, Ph.D. who ran that 24 year remote viewing project at SRI, which was funded by the CIA and DIA and much of their research is still classified. However, following are a couple of examples of their findings which have been declassified:

THE PAT PRICE CASE (July 1974): The CIA gave Hal Puthoff geographic coordinates of a location in West Virginia and asked if Stanford Research Institute (SRI) out in California could tell them what was located there, at a location 3000 miles away. Puthoff assigned the project to Pat Price. Price was a retired police detective who had used psychic powers to solve cases for years, and had responded to SRI's advertisements looking for sensitive people capable of remote viewing. Pat accepted the assignment and immediately sent in a five page report, which described a few log cabins and a couple of roads located at the specified geographic site and that was all he put in the report regarding the geographical co-ordinates which were given in the assignment. But, he added "Oh, by the way over the ridge there is this really interesting place. That must be the place you are actually interested in". He then went on to describe a secret military site he considered as being highly sensitive with the heaviest security. He provided code names related to the game of pool, along with other information about what was going on there and the personnel involved.

When the CIA got the report there primary reaction that it was way off and that the log cabins were merely the location of an Office of Scientific Intelligence (OSI) officer's vacation cabin. But, then a few days later when the OSI officer went out to the site he discovered that just over the ridge there was a highly sensitive underground government installation. The site was top secret and its existence totally a surprise to the CIA. Some of the details of the site were wrong, but a stunning number were right, including the code names relating to the game of pool which were used to identify files in a locked cabinet within the facility.

These kind of spectacular results cause a lot of interest in the military intelligence field, and Lt. Fredrick Atwater of the 902nd Military Intelligence Group at Ft. Meade, Maryland was drawn to these ideas. Lt. Atwater read a report published by William Braud,[79] associate professor of psychology at University of Houston, describing "psi conducive states". Atwater made a list of these traits and then combed through the personnel records of intelligence workers looking for people with these psi traits. He came up with Joe McMoneagle who was working as a senior projects officer for the U.S. Army Intelligence and Security Command (INSCOM) and after several interviews with Hal Puthoff and Russel Targ, McMoneagle was assigned by the Army to the SRI Remote Viewing Project.

THE JOE McMONEAGLE CASE (1979) – TYPHOON CLASS SUBMARINE: McMoneagle joined the SRI remote viewing project in 1978 and stayed for 18 years. Here is Hal Puthoff's description of Joe's work quoted from Elisabeth Mayer's book:[80]

"He'd produce masses of data that were really hot and totally inexplicable by ordinary means. One example that had particular impact on me was when Joe identified that the Russians were building a new form of submarine. Not only were the size and design judged by our military to be completely impossible. Worse was the fact that Joe said the Russians were building this huge submarine in the dead of a frozen Russian landscape with no direct access to water, so there would be no way to launch it. The whole thing seemed not just unlikely but crazy.

"It was during the fall of 1979 and it was one of the first operational targets we received once Joe was on board. A high-ranking naval officer from the Naval Security Council (NSC) brought us a photo of a massive, industrial-type building, some distance from a large body of water, located somewhere in Russia. The U.S. Government did not

know what the building was, what it was used for, or what its strategic importance was. It was unusual for its size and appeared to house a good deal of activity so they wanted to know more.

"We gave Joe the geographic coordinates, nothing else. His immediate response was that they identified a very cold wasteland with an extremely large industrial-looking building that had enormous smokestacks, not far from a sea covered with a thick cap of ice. Later, we found out the location was Sverodvinsk on the White Sea.

"Since the first quick impression corresponded very closely to the photograph, we showed Joe the picture and asked what might be going on inside it. Here's his own retrospective account of the viewing:

"I spent some time relaxing and emptying my mind. Then with my eyes closed, I imagined myself drifting down into the building, passing downward through its roof. What I found was mind-blowing. The building was easily the size of two or three huge shopping centers, all under a single roof......

"In giant bays between the walls were what looked like cigars of different sizes sitting in gigantic racks.... Thick masses of scaffolding and interlocking steel pipes were everywhere. Within these were what appeared to be two huge cylinders being welded side to side, and I had an overwhelming sense that this was a submarine, a really big one, with twin hulls.....

"What I didn't know was that my session was reported back to the NSC and created some dissension. The almost unanimous belief at the time, by all the intelligence collection agencies operating against the building, was that the Soviets were constructing a brand new type of assault ship—a troop carrier, and possibly one with helicopter capability. A submarine was out of the question.

"On my second visit, I got up very close .... Hovering beside it, I guessed it to be about twice the length of an American football field and nearly seventy feet in width, and at least six or seven floors high (if it were sitting next to a standard apartment building). It was clearly constructed of two huge elongated tubes run side-by-side for almost it's entire length. (I didn't think this was possible with submarines) ..... I moved up over the deck and was surprised to see that it had canted missile tubes running side by side. This was critically important because this indicated that it had the capacity to fire while on the move rather than having to stand still in the water, which made it a very dangerous type of submarine....

After this session I did a very detailed drawing of the submarine, adding dimensions, as well as noting the slanted tubes, indicating eighteen to twenty in all. This material, along with the typed transcript of my session....was forwarded to .... The NSC...

We soon received a follow on request... to return to the target and try to provide an estimated time of completion....

I revisited the site and, based on the speed of construction and the differences in the condition of the submarine from one session to the next, I guessed that it would be ready for launch about four months later—that would be sometime in the month of January (1980) A singularly crazy time of year to launch a submarine from a building not connected to water, near a sea frozen over with ice yards thick. (I reported that very soon a crew of bulldozers and other types of heavy equipment would arrive to cut a channel leading to the sea).

Recognizance photos taken by US satellite in January 1980 showed a new canal running alongside the building and out to the White Sea. Also in the photos was clearly a two hulled submarine with 20 missile tubes. This was the first of the Typhoon class of submarine, the largest submarines ever built. And, it was exactly what Joe McMoneagle had described.

There are many books on the market which describe the SRI remote viewing projects in great detail, especially now that about half of the Top Secret records have been declassified. It is really a hot topic among people on the cutting edge of scientific exploration. If you want to know more about remote viewing, I do recommend reading Elizabeth Mayer's book *Extraordinary Knowing*, which covers all of this in greater detail.

Remote viewing is merely a process of getting the consciousness channel tuned with the will channel within an individuals mind. What McMoneagel called "Shutting down my conscious mind", is this turning down of the noise in Walker's consciousness channel, in order to access through the p-car established by the two channels all the shared fragments of mind experience, which have been added to the earth's limitless data storage system (Akashic record).

STAGGERING CONCLUSIONS:

Finally, taking this all together we find inescapably that everything we each *believe* that we see is merely the *illusion* that we are mentally projecting as our universe. What we each see as "reality" is merely the illusion we choose to sketch on the veil. This reality is entirely constructed of thoughts, and these are actually shared thoughts so that like schools of fish, which suddenly turn together, the habitual perceptive fields of our surrounding culture causes those around us, through habit, to project a similar reality. So that we behold similar illusions (shared reality). It is only when we lift the veil that we can see the true reality which in my opinion can most easily be stated as:

"We are our thoughts, and our thoughts are the Universe."

Following is a paraphrase of the leading physicist, former Astronaut (Edgar Mitchell) in which he says this same thing:

THE PERMANENT RECORD (Quantum Hologram, or Akashic Record)

"The underlying scientific case for mind to mind and mind to matter communications has been impressively well documented by several rigorous studies of these phenomenon, i.e. Princeton Engineering Anomalies Research (PEAR), Stanford Research Institute (SRI), University of Virginia, and University of Arizona. These ongoing studies conducted over many decades provide compelling results showing staggering probabilities against chance.

"Consequently, this non-local quantum hologram, which is based on sound theory and recently verified through the practical application of fMRI, provides sufficient rigorous proof to postulate the theory that the quantum hologram is, in fact, a macro-scale, non-local, information structure (Akashic Record), which extends quantum mechanics to encompass all physical objects including DNA molecules, organic cells, organs, brains and bodies

*"Further, the storage and transmission of non-local correlations and non-local quantum information can now be seen to be ubiquitous throughout the universe....such that the quantum hologram can properly be labeled as "nature's mind" and that **the intuitive function we label in humans as the "sixth sense" or "second sight" should properly be called the "first sense".***

"Any complex evolved organism which can form an intent (idea or wish) can, in fact, produce and often do produce non-local causal effects associated with that specific intent. Further, it has been found that attention alone produces coherence in nature (resonant relationship, P-car, quantum coherence) that in some measure reduces randomness.

"Finally, it can be postulated that non-locality in the universe is the antecedent attribute of energy and matter, which both allows perception and is also the root of the consciousness, which manifests in the evolved organisms existing in three dimensional reality."

EVOLUTIONARY FEED BACK LOOP: *"The discovery of the quantum hologram as a solution which seems to resolve so many phenomena, points to the logical conclusion that classical theory is incomplete unless it includes the subtle non-local components so deeply involved. This suggests that a major paradigm shift is now forthcoming in our 21st century scientific ontology.*

*"Papers published by Marcer and Schempp propose a learning model both for DNA and prokaryote cells using quantum holography, and further suggest that evolution in general is driven by a learning feedback loop with the environment, rather than progressing through random mutations as postulated in Darwinian theories. **This same solution to biological evolution was originally proposed by Lamarck in 1809, but was discarded by 19th century materialist scientists in favor of the clockwork mechanistic solution of random mutations suggested by Darwin".***

Former Astronaut Edgar Mitchell's conclusions regarding the Quantum Hologram. Mitchell is a consciousness researcher and founder of the Institute of Noetic Sciences (IONS)

WHAT THIS MEANS:

Literally, all the information that ever was is actually stored throughout the universe, and can be accessed by those who have psychic abilities (i.e. can tune into the P-car signals). Also, each of us materializes instantaneously and continually a holographic energy projection from the dark energy into this light energy. The following quotation is from the founder of Quantum Mechanics (parenthetical inclusions are my own interpretations):

"Inconceivable as it seems to ordinary reason, you–and all other conscious beings, as such, are the all in all.

(The soul of the conscious universe).

"Hence this life of yours, which you are living is not merely a piece of the entire existence, but is in a certain sense the whole.....Thus you can throw yourself flat on the ground, stretched out upon Mother Earth, with the certain conviction that you are one with her and she with you. You are as firmly established, as invulnerable as she, indeed a thousand times firmer and more invulnerable. As surely as she will engulf you tomorrow, so surely will she bring you forth anew to new striving and suffering. And, not merely "someday":

"Now, today, every day she is bringing you forth, not once but thousands upon thousands of times, just as every day she engulfs you a thousand times over ......"[81]

Erwin Schrödinger, founder of quantum mechanics

The ZPF continually generates the specific energy that perpetuates the illusion of the matter that is you,......

"You move your hand and the universe carries out the subtle energy transformations from dark energy to light energy that constantly supports the holographic illusion of matter which is you here in space-time, and continues to instantaneously recreate the hologram of your hand in the moving positions and gives you the illusion of movement..... you think and the universe performs the particle physics "magic" to make it so. "[81]

Erwin Schrödinger, founder of quantum mechanics

The above quotation is not from a medieval Christian Mystic, but is from one of the greatest scientific minds of the 20th century. From the very mind which created quantum mechanics. He realizes that each of us is part of the whole. Each of us is an integral part of the conscious universe and inseparable from it.

Here is another quotation showing how another great scientific thinker sees the same phenomena:

"Up to now we have been looking at matter as such, that is to say according to its qualities and in any given volume—as though it were permissible for us to break off a fragment and

> *study this sample apart from the rest. It is time to point out that this procedure is merely an intellectual dodge. Considered in its physical concrete reality....the universe can not divide itself but, as a kind of gigantic "atom" it forms in its totality....the only real indivisible....The farther and more deeply we penetrate into matter, by means of increasingly powerful methods, the more we are confounded by the interdependence of its parts. Each element of the cosmos is positively woven from all the others....It is impossible to cut into this network, to isolate a portion without it becoming frayed and unraveled at all its edges. All around us, as far as the eye can see, the universe holds together, and only one way of considering it is really possible, that is to take it as a whole in one piece."[82]*
>
> Pierre Teilhard de Chardin

And, yes this time the quote is from a Christian Mystic, but one who is also a world renowned 20th century paleontologist. Yet, both quotations; one from a physicist and one from a Christian mystic paleontologist are striking at exactly the same chord, i.e.

"We (each of us) are not separate from the whole".

This is a philosophical application of non-locality, which shows that we as individuals are not separate from the Conscious Universe.

CONCLUSION:

If consciousness (mind and soul) can move from one body to the next, as experienced daily through transplant surgery, and if the entire universe is one conscious whole, as postulated by quantum mechanics, then the individual conscious mind must actually exist totally outside the body, and is merely perceived to actually be in the body. In other words,

"Your consciousness (mind) is actually out-of-body right now, you just habitually choose to perceive it to be inside your body".

REBUTTAL:

Unfortunately, the prevailing trend in physics education even today does not teach any sort of view which gives primacy to formative activity in undivided wholeness. Yet, such a perspective is necessary to support the above conclusions. Instead, most physics education de-emphasizes those aspects of relativity theory and quantum theory which suggest the need for such an undivided wholeness perspective of reality. Consequently, most physics students regard these "problem areas" as merely being obscure aspects of mathematical calculus and not as being indicators of the real nature of things.

Also, most physicists still speak and think in terms of the traditional 19th century atomistic notion that the universe is constituted of elementary particles which are the "basic building blocks" out of which everything is made. Consequently, when evidence is presented that tends to disprove their basic world view they tend to either minimize its significance or simply ignore it. For a deeper discussion of this problem, with perception on the nature of reality, please read *Wholeness and the Implicate Order* ©1980 by David Bohm (1917-1992).[83]

If you wish to learn more about all of this new science try listening to the following talks which describe many of the PSI experiments which have verified much of the consciousness effects:

Dean Radin, Senior scientist at Institute of Noetic Sciences (IONS), speaking on <u>Science and the Taboo of PSI</u> at:
http://www.youtube.com/watch?v=qv_09Qiwqew

Dean Radin, speaking on <u>Consciousness, Photons & RNpRWpkeality</u> at:
• Part 1/5 http;//www.youtube.com/watch?v=6tjvpk_x-YI
• Part 2/5 http;//www.youtube.com/watch?v=zrxqz
• Part 3/5 http;//www.youtube.com/watch?v=IBDmHT-D5bs
• Part 4/5 http;//www.youtube.com/watch?v=44OaMnw-Sx8
• Part 5/5 http;//www.youtube.com/watch?v=FmxFsxB_H40

CHAPTER 7

THE WEIGHING OF THE HEART

La pesée du coeur"

"… man is destined to die once,
and after that to face judgment."
Hebrews 9:27 (NIV)

THE NEAR DEATH EXPERIENCE LIFE REVIEW:

One of the most intriguing things to come out of the recent studies of the Near-Death experience (**NDE**) is the persistent occurrence of the *Life Review*. This *weighing of the heart*, which occurs in accounts of hundreds of NDE's, provides the participant with a review of all the significant events of their lifetime and occurs shortly after their consciousness has left the physical body. Immediately after conclusion of this life review the NDE continues with an important question which takes this form,

> **"Was it enough?"** or **"Have you learned enough that you are ready to move on?"**

If the answer is "No", and the deceased individual still has unfinished business in the prior life, then the decision is made to return to that prior life, and reincarnate in the same body. Apparently, if the answer is YES, then the person moves on into the afterlife because no one who answered, "YES" has returned to the prior life to report an NDE.

THE ANCIENT MYTH OF A LAST JUDGEMENT, "La pesée du coeur":

Ancient accounts of the NDE, many of which include a life review, have been discovered throughout written literature as far back as 2500 BC, and include several NDE's recorded by highly revered early Christian fathers (See chapter 3). It is evident from this ancient literature that civilizations knew of NDE's nearly 5000 years ago, as did the early Christians in those centuries before the Roman emperors began to impose the dark ages and a thousand years of illiterate "group think" onto western Christianity after 390 AD. Finally the emperor outlawed belief in NDE's and transmigration (reincarnation) after 553AD. But, these ancient NDE accounts clearly agree with the modern NDE of the 21st century, all telling the same story of what lies beyond the grave.

On the other hand, Joseph Campbell suggests that knowledge of things beyond the grave may actually be a part of the greater gnosis which informs all cultures through intuition. This shared gnosis residing in a memory storage field which Carl Jung named the *collective unconscious* causes the myths to reappear in all cultures throughout history.

"And so, indeed, it does appear that anyone viewing with unprejudiced eye the religions of mankind must recognize mythic themes at every hand that are shared, though differently interpreted, among the peoples of the planet. James G. Frazer, in *The Golden Bough*, thought to explain such correspondences simply as, 'The effect of similar causes acting alike on the similar constitution of the human mind in different countries and under different skies'. Bastian,...characterizes them as *elementary ideas*, and Carl G. Jung... proposed his theory of *arch types of the consciousness*".

Joseph Campbell, p. 80 *The Inner Reaches of Outerspace* ©1984

THE ANCIENT EGYPTIAN WEIGHING OF THE HEART:

On my desk there is a print of an ancient Egyptian papyrus entitled *la Pesée du Coeur* the original is held in Paris at the Louvre. The papyrus Illustrates, "The Weighing of the Heart" (*la Pesée du Coeur*). and shows the ancient Egyptian myth of the last judgment, the philosophy of which has been documented in surviving written artifacts from as far back as 4500 years ago (2500 BC),[84] and considering that remnants of this same ancient myth appear even earlier in the Bahgavad Gita, dated by scholars around 3000 BC (and archeo-astrologically dated to as early as 5561 BC), the myth portrayed in the papyrus is at least 5000 years old and may be vastly older. Obviously it is basic part of mankind's inner psyche as understood by Jung and Campbell.

This ancient myth also contains all the significant beliefs of most modern religions (Christian, Moslem, Jewish, Hindu & Buddhist). Yet, the myth is obviously describing **the same** *life review* **reported by the 21st century NDE,** which examines how the recently deceased feels about all the events that transpired in their immediately prior life. Here is that Papyrus with an explanation following that describes the weighing of the heart.

La pesée du Coeur
Photo by Author

La pesée du coeur

The papyrus shows the goddess Maat, who represents the divine attributes of truth, honesty, justice and fairness. She is observing a balance scale which is weighing the heart of a disincarnate individual who is recently deceased. On the other side of the balance, being weighed against the heart is Maat's feather of righteousness. Maat holds in her left hand the key of life (ankh), ready to award it to this deceased person if she finds the weight of their heart to be "light as a feather"

*(i.e. She is asking him whether his experiences in the physical life have given him enough trials, tribulations and lessons to achieve the growth necessary for his spirit to finally be at peace so that his heart is therefore ligh*t).

Standing on a pedestal on the side of the deceased, and shown as a monkey, is Horus, the Son of the God (Osiris). Horus is himself a God who was born of a virgin (immaculate conception). His mother, Isis was impregnated by the spirit (Holy Ghost) of the deceased god Osiris. Horus is actually waiting to tilt the scale in favor of the deceased. This *Son of God* is ready to literally "make up for the sins of the deceased".

TWO POSSIBLE OUTCOMES:
If the deceased's heart is not weighted down with the burden of sin, then Maat will give the key of life and the deceased will travel on into the heavens to the star Sirius (Isis) and Orion (Osiris) to rejoin the god's from which he came, and live with them in the heavens eternally, having

after many lifetimes escaped the wheel of repeated lives and finally achieved Buddha-hood.

On the other hand, if his heart is still weighted down with the burdens of this life, then his experiences in the physical life have not brought him enough pain to garner the gnosis necessary to no longer care about the things of this physical existence in time and space. And therefore, because his heart is still heavy he will have to travel back through the underworld led by the guide dog Anuket to be "Born again" and reincarnate as a human for another physical lifetime of seeking wisdom from the trials of physical life.

ALL AFTERLIFE SALVATION MYTHS BEGAN HERE:

This papyrus is clearly describing the life review portion of the Near-Death experience. So, it is then obvious that the surviving parts of the ancient Egyptian legend depicted in the papyrus which still appear in the salvation myths of each of the world's religions came from prior knowledge of the NDE.

CHRISTIAN LAST JUDGMENT: For example, the Christians believe that after death there is a final judgment where Christ, who like Horus in the papyrus is believed to be the Son of God born of a virgin, makes up for your sins. At the Christian *Last Judgment*, if you are found righteous you are given the, "crown of life" (the ankh), and you then go to be with God (Isis & Osiris) in the heavens (the stars Sirius & Orion). But, if your sins are too great (i.e. your heart is too heavy) and you don't seek help from Christ (or Horus) to tip the balance in your favor (propitiation) then you are condemned to go down into the underworld (Hades or hell). The only part of the Egyptian myth which is missing from today's Christian version of the salvation myth is the opportunity for rebirth into another physical life (reincarnation), otherwise, the 21th century Christian salvation myth is identical to the ancient Egyptian afterlife myth, but with the addition of retribution, hellfire and damnation in the underworld which has been transformed into a place of eternal retribution.

Twentieth century biblical scholarship on early Christianity has shown that reincarnation was the accepted doctrine in early Christianity. It is now well documented that reincarnation was taught by the early Christian fathers including Origen of Alexandria (185-254 AD) who is considered one of the greatest of the early Christian theologians (see also chapter 4).

NOTE: This means that the theology of the early Christian church of the first century, which included reincarnation in their original Christian Salvation Myth, was IDENTICAL to the ancient Egyptian Salvation Myth from 2450 years earlier.

Further, the Christian religion of biblical times was a reawakening of ancient enlightenment of Thoth-Hermes in the Hebrew community much as it was already being practiced in the Hellenistic Mystery religions throughout the known world for at least 500 years before Christ[85]. This so called "new" Christian religion was merely a rebranding of the pre-existing "pagan" religion, as clearly stated by Christian Bishop Saint Augustine (November 13, 354 AD – August 28, 430 AD):

> *"That which is called the "Christian" religion existed among the ancients, and never did not exist, from the beginning of the human race until Christ came in the flesh, at which time the true religion WHICH ALREADY EXISTED began to be called Christianity"*[86]
>
> St. Augustine, *Retractions*, Taken from P.54 *The Fathers of the Church, Saint Augustine, The Retractions.* Brogan ©1968, Catholic University of America Press. Augustine's Retractions were written as a clarification in 428 AD, after publication of his seminal work the City of God in 427AD)[2]

Given the above documented facts honest science causes one to ask, "How did the original salvation myth get so grievously altered and why? Here is that history.

THE SINGLE LIFE THEORY: Unfortunately, politics has always been the force behind any form of "organized" religion. 125 years after St. Augustine the Christian salvation myth was drastically reduced by the Roman emperor in order to allow only a single physical life. In 553AD at the Fifth Ecumenical Council (2nd Council at Constantinople), which was called by Emperor Justinian and not the sitting Pope, that the doctrines of Origen regarding reincarnation were ostracized.[87] The Pope even refused to attend this council, and it was Justinian who pushed for this rejection of reincarnation. Yet, the adoption of these "Anathemas against Origen", which ostracized those who believed in reincarnation, were never recorded in the official minutes of this ecumenical council. So it appears that the attending bishops did not want to grant the Emperor's desires. However, Justinian claimed that these anathemas were in fact adopted at the council and set about enforcing this change in doctrine and belief throughout the Roman Empire. Anyone who disagreed was simply killed. Next, where Jesus had clearly spoken in the canon gospels about multiple lifetimes the church now had to reinterpret his remarks. Instead of multiple lifetimes to work on your karma and get it right with God, a Christian believer now had to be spiritually "born again" in the same physical body during that single lifetime. But, now add to this Original Sin.

ORIGINAL SIN: Earlier, in the late 4th and early 5th centuries Roman Catholics had added the new idea of guilt called *Original Sin* and along with it the idea of retribution or *Eternal Damnation* (Hell) as a punishment for sinners. There are no scriptural or historic records for the existence of these beliefs in the four hundred years of Christianity prior to that time. Yet now, taken together these two ideas, only one life and retribution for sin in the afterlife, gave the Roman emperors through the church great power to successfully control the populace through religion.

The Roman church also claimed the power of the *Office of the Keys,* saying that God had given the Roman church the power of retaining a person's sins against him, even though he may have repented. The church could now, by simply refusing to allow forgiveness, deny a person eternal life in heaven, and force them to suffer the eternal damnation of burning in hell.

MUSLIM'S ALSO BELIEVE IN A LAST JUDGEMENT: The Muslim beliefs about death and the afterlife, formulated by Mohammad in the 7th century, a hundred years after Emperor Justinian had literally "killed off" all beliefs in reincarnation, naturally retained the same *Single Life Theory,* but unlike the Christians, with no savior (Horus/Christ) and no rebirth in this life. Instead, Muslims believe you must do all atonement yourself in one lifetime by preforming the five pillars of the Islamic faith, and in the Day of Judgment (*weighing of the heart*) if your good deeds outweigh bad deeds then you go to live with God in paradise.

> *NOTE: Within Islam there are two small Shiite sects, which still believe in reincarnation or takamous.[88] These are the Druse of Lebanon and Syria and the Alevis of Turkey, similar to Sufi Muslims all are regarded as not being truly Muslim by other sects of Islam. Consequently, they have been continually harried and killed by both the Shiite and Sunni sects for over 1300 years.*

HINDU & BUDDHIST SALVATION MYTHS LACK A LAST JUDGEMENT: In the East, both Hindu and Buddhist salvation myths retain the numerous lifetimes of reincarnation, The Hindu's retain a form of the *Weighing of the Heart,* believing that after a person dies a supernatural being Brahman (Maat) weighs the good and evil done by that person and assigns them their next place of reincarnation. Brahman can mitigate the negative effect of early mistakes in life if later in life many good deeds were done. In Buddhist thinking which is an off-shoot of Hindu beliefs, there is no actual *Weighing of the Heart,* but, the soul cannot escape the "wheel of repeated lifetimes" until it is worthy of Buddha-hood, and this

123

attained level of purification amounts to the same result as the *Weighing of the Heart.*

COMPARISON OF RELIGIOUS SALVATION MYTH BELIEFS:

ORIGINAL EGYPTIAN

CURRENT AFTERLIFE BELIEFS OF MAJOR RELIGIONS

AFTERLIFE BELIEF ELEMENT	CHRISTIAN	MUSLIM	HINDU	BUDDHIST
1. Belief in Afterlife/Eternal life	YES	YES	YES	YES
2. Belief in Universal Salvation	NO	NO	YES	YES
3. Belief in Final Judgment	YES	YES	YES	NO
4. Belief in Crown of Life (Ankh) And going to live with God	YES	YES	YES	YES
5. Belief in Savior (Christ/Horus)	YES	NO	NO	NO
6. Belief in **REINCARNATION** [a,b]	NO	NO	YES	YES
7. Belief in Hell/Hades/underworld	YES	YES	NO	NO
ADD-ON BELIEFS				
8. Belief in Eternal Damnation	YES	YES	NO	NO

[a] Modern Christians misinterpret reincarnation to be "Born Again" which means having the Spirit "re-born" in the same physical body during a single physical life lived in the" one lifetime hypothesis".

[b] Two small Muslim sects do believe in reincarnation.

THE MISSING PIECES: Today, bringing back into the Christian salvation myth the knowledge which the Near-Death experience provides about transmigration of the consciousness (out of body reincarnation) and also that the awareness that the life review includes no retribution would make Christianity identical with the ancient Egyptian religion. This restoration of reincarnation would also allow future lifetimes in which Muslims could continue to improve their karma by following the five pillars of the faith. This also allows both Christians and Muslims to accept past life memories, which is the subject of chapter 4.

PART 2

THE ROAD MAP

CHAPTER 8

FACING DEATH

1. GETTING PREPARED FOR THE JOURNEY

Forgetting the speculative beliefs about the afterlife that you may have heard from all the traditional religions and even the medical community, and instead considering the collected evidence outlined in the prior chapters, which current replicated research of the afterlife has verified, and you may now realize that....... **Death is not final, and therefore your consciousness (you) will not cease to exist**.

Additionally, it is not necessary to give your life savings to the church of your choice or some other worthy cause in order to pay for your sins in this life. It appears from the collected evidence that the entire concept of sin and retribution is a simple misunderstanding and that you literally have a free ticket to move on from this physical life into the next phase.

The truth is that, **your consciousness is simply going to move on to a new plane of existence where you will continue to have additional experiences.**

In fact, the death penalty (capital punishment), which westerners think might be the ultimate punishment for criminals, may actually be a wonderful reprieve for them. Just consider how Saint Paul's words from the canon (approved) New Testament ring true:

"to die is gain".
St. Paul, Philippians 1:21

THE REAL FEAR: What everyone really fears about death, is what we all intrinsically know in our very bones. We know that there *is* an

126

afterlife and that we do not merely cease to exist forever. But, we also believe from our religions that there may be a judgment in the afterlife that will have to be reckoned with. Pascal made a famous wager:

"If we become nothing after death, we will not be there to regret having prepared for something. On the other hand, if we are something after death, and we have not prepared for it at all, or are badly prepared, then we will feel bitter, painful regret for a very long time. So, we have everything to lose by not preparing, and nothing to gain; and we have everything to gain by preparing and nothing to lose. Should our preparation be for nought, a little time spent on it in this life will not be regretted for eternity."

Pascal

In any case, it is simply irrational as a human to set out on a journey to that undiscovered country unprepared and without a road map.

NOTHING TO FEAR: But, while it is human to fear, the afterlife science of the Near-Death experience has begun to show that the judgment, or life review (weighing of the heart), is only a learning process and not a trial. Indeed, while it may take place in the presence of the being of light (Christ / Maat), and you may re-live all the experiences of your life, complete with the feelings and emotions of those who were with you in each event, this is only done so that you can determine whether the life just ended was *worth it*, and whether or not you got from this lifetime what it was that you came to earth to get. And, if during this *weighing of the heart* you find that the trials and tribulations have given you the lessons you came to get, then the *Final Judgment* you will personally pronounce on this life is that, "It was good"

"For we shall all appear before the judgment seat of Christ; that everyone may receive the things done in his body, according to that which he has done." St. Paul, who had experienced his own Near-Death experience is here describing the life review in 2 Corinthians 5:10 (KJV)

And you will move on to the next phase. The important thing to grasp is that:

Death is not to be feared. It is just another part of your continuing travels. Consider it more like a way station where you rest before starting the next leg of the continuing journey.

APPROACHING DEATH with the TERMINALLY ILL

For many people who are terminally ill and approaching death it becomes easier as they get closer to it. Many who are close to death have had a Near-Death type experience prior to the final phase of their illness. However, these experiences occurring as death approaches during our final days are called Nearing-Death awareness or Near-Death approaches (NDAs)[89] These experiences are similar to, and yet profoundly different from the Near-Death experience (NDE).

These NDAs often take place without any sudden shift in physical condition which normally coincides with an NDE. They most often include meeting deceased relatives, and seem to be a form of preparation for death. The overall experience seems to be quite reassuring. NDAs can occur when the person is fully conscious. The patient may be able to move back and forth from the afterlife back into the present reality, talking with dead relatives on the other side, and then re-focusing here in this reality to begin talking to those attending them bedside, literally bridging the gap between two alternative realities at once. They may say that they see a deceased loved one sitting in the chair across the room (but which none of the attending family can see). Yet, it is obvious to the attending family that the one preparing to depart is not hallucinating, but is actually perceiving on both sides of the veil. During these NDA's the departing loved one is fully conscious of both the present reality and the other side at the same time. They easily pay attention to what is happening in the hospital room, as well as to their visiting spirits. Therefore, by definition, these experiences are not hallucinations. Such NDA's differ markedly from an hallucination. People experiencing hallucinations cannot suspend their hallucinatory reality momentarily in order to converse with people in this reality. On-the-other-hand people having an NDA can differentiate between the two realities. So, it appears instead that these experiences are more likely, exactly what they seem to be, actual visitations from the out-of-body consciousness of deceased relatives.

One phenomena which illustrates that the NDA is a visitation from the other side is the fact that living relatives who are absent from the hospital room never seem to be perceived among the visitors from the other side, by the dying person. But, several cases have been reported and verified where spirits are observed as deceased persons, yet whom the patient believed until that moment were still alive. Later, it is confirmed that the "unexpected" deceased spirits had indeed died unbeknown to the patient, which is why they appear in the group of visitors from the other side.

The dying patient can take great comfort from these visitation experiences if they are reassured by the attendants that their experiences are perfectly normal at this stage of life.

LAST CHORES – GETTING READY TO MAKE AN EXIT: Patients approaching death are faced with several tasks, which may not occur to be relevant to those attending them. While the attendants are worrying about the impending death, funerals, relatives, medical bills, taxes, etc. the dying patient may instead be consciously reviewing the life they have lived. To them this is now vastly more important than our day to day concerns. Sometimes their review is done in great detail, with the greatest interest involving their relationships. They may be looking for themes in their lives and maybe for the first time asking the question, "What was it all for?" They may want to identify what they have learned and what they have contributed. At this point forgiveness becomes a major concern. Facing death they realize that forgiveness for what they have done, and forgiving others for what they did to them is an important part of their unfinished business.

They also begin the process of saying good-by to all the familiar parts of this life. They start to let go of things, one at a time....... *"I guess I won't be making that trip to Asia now?"....... "Maybe I should leave the farm to Clyde since he would have more time for it than his more successful brother George?"...." Who will be the Santa at the Lodge Christmas party after I am gone?"..... "I wonder whatever happened to Richard who fought with me in the South Pacific?"......Or, "What about Mark my seventh grade boy friend, last I heard he had four children?".......*

HOW TO COMMUNICATE WITH THE DYING:

As you prepare for your own death, some of your immediate family and friends may begin to make the journey before you, and you will be called upon to attend them in their last hours. Be straightforward and honest in your communications, but do let them lead the way. You still have time to get your affairs in order, but they are short of time so let them be "in charge".

They may talk about starting a journey to that undiscovered country, or getting ready to go home. For example:

A bereaved widow told me that during her husband's last days he would be collecting his things together, and she would ask him,

"Where are you going". He would always answer, "I'm *going home"*. She did not know what to think because they were home in the house he had built for her some 50 years earlier, but there he was packing his things to go to some other home.

As he continued to "get ready to go" this way day after day, she finally said to him, *"Don't you like it here in the home you built?"* And he answered, *"This is not my real home.....And, I understand that you still like it here in this home, because you aren't ready to go home yet, But, I am leaving"*.

So, it is important to be sensitive to their needs regarding: how close they want you to sit, how much company they want, and how much talking is comfortable for them. Simply let them be "in charge" as much as possible. Often, gently holding their hand may be the most comfortable, and all they need. If they have had an NDE or NDA allow them to talk about it, and be ready to believe what they report to you, knowing that what they are perceiving as real, *is real* even if you can't see it at the same time, or even if it disagrees markedly with what you church wants you to believe. Just allow their experience to be real.

Realize that as death approaches, they may need to withdraw into themselves to contemplate deep thoughts during the process of saying good-by to this life. Often, they may be distracted, deep in thought and unable to focus on family members or what is going on around them. Also, they may not want to visit as much with loved ones as they did before.

When this is the case, do not have your feelings hurt. Just understand that they may need time alone as a necessary part of their preparation for their journey into death.

CHOOSING THE MOMENT: Contrary to popular belief, the dying often have the ability to choose the actual moment of dying and some people actually want to die when their loved ones are out of the room. Some people simply find it easier to let go when they are alone. Often, families misunderstand this need for solitude and feel, quite unnecessarily, guilty that they weren't there at the exact moment of death.

If they are waiting for a significant relative or friend to come to the bedside, terminally ill people may remain close to death for a long period of time even days or weeks just to complete unfinished business with those relatives before making their transition into spirit.

On the other hand, many dying people like to have someone with them, yet they may not wish to (or be able to) interact very much. Your quiet presence may be all that they want. Know that this last stage of life often provides the most powerful interactions that loved ones will have in their entire lifetime.

My personal goal is to have a conscious death at home, and not at the hospital. This is a rarity in today's American culture. But, I will choose when I will die, and I will go at the correct time, without attempting to prolong my earthly life by artificial means. I will go in conscious awareness welcoming the start of my final journey from this current physical life to that marvelous undiscovered country. Bon Voyage.

APPARITIONS AND NOTIFICATIONS:

After the patient has died, it is not uncommon for surviving loved ones to sense the presence of the departed relative. Some people who were not present for the death may feel that they were notified of the death by the person who has just died through an apparition or other communication. This may take the form of a visitation during a dream. Bereaved people often report various forms of visitation and communication. Unfortunately, our Western culture tends to reject these as imaginative yearnings of bereaved hearts rather that admitting that they could actually be real and honest experiences.

The bereaved often feel the presence of their recently deceased loved ones who seem to be checking in on them. They may hear words, see their image, smell a familiar aroma such as a favorite shaving lotion, or merely sense their presence. Also, deceased loved ones may alert friends or family about some impending danger. Such continuing contact with the deceased is not only usual it is also quite normal.

WHERE DO WE GO, WHAT DOES IT LOOK LIKE?

The Buddhist descriptions of the stages of the death process roughly agree with the experience of the NDE. The colors which the Buddhist tradition describes do match the colors that I saw personally. Further, the Buddhist death process describes the final arrival into a very transparent out-of-body consciousness that is so subtle it cannot be seen by untrained eyes of medical personnel or relatives attending the death. It is what is sometimes called the ghost essence. NDE researchers continue to report that this essence is indeed there, present near the body which they have now left behind.

NDE accounts speak of being in the upper area of the room, and similar details are given in the recorded memories of the time "between lives" by re-incarnated children. Many Near-Death survivors speak of their journey in this spirit essence, near the top of the room, and even through walls and doors or outside on the roof above the hospital. In one story (related elsewhere in this text) a man remembers spending seven years in a tree, as one of these ghost essences (See the Bongkuch Promsin Case in chapter 4).

CHAPTER 9

BEGINNING THE JOURNEY

LEAVING FOR THE UNDISCOVERED COUNTRY

This description of the stages in the death process follows a sequence synthesized from the multiple sources including:

1. The Tibetan book of the dead[1]
2. The Egyptian book of the dead
3. Dr. Moody's "standard" Near-Death experience[90]
4. My own Near-Death experience (see chapter 3) including my passage out-of-body to the other side.
5. Dr. Hossack's description related posthumously to Edward C. Randall[91] as an After Death Communication. (see chapter 5)

   The sequence also agrees with my own personal remembrances of the stages of my near death experience and my passage out-of-body on the other side. This description is tempered with what I have learned from other Near-Death experiencers during my years of association with the *International Association for Near-Death Studies* (IANDS), especially the publications of P.H.M.Atwater, and my own research into the Hermetica, the non-local universe of quantum mechanics, and the 120 years of scientific study by the British *Society for Psychical Research* (SPR), and the *American Society for Psychical Research* (ASPR), and the Spiritualitst of the Morris Pratt Institute.

This description is not based on mere religious beliefs or speculations, but is entirely based on first hand remembered, reported and researched facts. This description is a synthesis of the gnosis from each of these perspectives, guided by my own first hand knowing of the journey itself as well as eyewitness accounts of others. It is also arranged to show how the death process will occur for the average conscious individual, without the interference of drugs or other modern medical procedures which are mistakenly designed to stave off our experience of death itself.

WHAT DYING IS LIKE

ONE DAY IT'S TIME TO GO: This could all happen quickly if you are killed in an accident. But, it happens more slowly with a natural death. After a period of struggle with the decision whether to stay here or to go, your consciousness (soul) decides to depart from the flesh. For some hours or days prior to this point you may have been catching fleeting glimpses of the other side.[92] You may have heard what you thought were angels singing, or had distinct visions of dead relatives on the other-side, etc.

> "*It is inconceivable to the conscious mind* (that another place could exist) *besides the earth world of matter bounded by time and space* (3-D)....*Instinctively, you fight to live.....*[93]
> P.H.M. Atwater, a multiple NDE survivor describing the mind's reaction upon first arriving on the other side.

Yet, peace awaits you and so you cease the tiring efforts of holding this earthly illusion of time and space together. You feel weak and sinking, melting back into spirit from the physicality of this material reality. Your body seems to get smaller (shrivel) as the reflection of opposites (positive & negative) what Buddhists call mirror-wisdom, which is the transmuted energy of this earthly delusion, dissolves. Forms of matter become indistinct, the vision and eye perception deteriorates and all sights are blurred. Things begin to appear like the mirage of water in the distance on a highway. This condition may persist for hours or days. In this apparent delirium you may see former relatives or angels beckoning you from the other side of the veil. You may be speaking to them, while also coming back to speak with those here on this side of the veil. There is no clear edge to the veil any longer, there is the other side (reality) with the light where your deceased loved ones are waiting, and yet there is still this physical illusion in time and space where your living loved ones are going to be left behind. Nostalgia mixes with anticipation. A better future beckons, but you hesitate to leave behind these living loved ones. Truly, parting is such sweet sorrow. But, by now you know you want to go and so you start saying, "good bye". Some relatives are pleading with you not to go, others are wondering, "How does he know it's his time?" You call for certain people, and so decide to wait another 24 or 48 hours for them to come so you can say your good byes to them as well.

Then you finally make your exit. Slowly, the water dissolves into fire, and the bodily fluids seem to dry out, sensations cease as you become numb, equalizing your wisdom as you no longer have to remain in attachment to the physical body. Your energy is pulling back into its subtle essence. All feelings, pain and emotion melt away as sensations disappear. Hearing goes, yet not necessarily, the sense of understanding. You will begin to pick up the thoughts of others now without necessarily hearing their words. ESP is better attuned now that you aren't dependent upon the physical senses and your true thoughts are no longer drowned out by the "noise" of bodily sensations. This "second sight" or increased intuition which is the tool of mediums and clairvoyants has once again become a sharp sense for you too. Many Near-Death survivors heard conversations clearly, even when well beyond this point and completely out-of-body. But that is also the state where communication is received in images rather than sounds. We Near-Death experiencers say that, "The Being of Light spoke to us, but not in words per se, we just received the message".

Truly the most frustrating thing as you go deeper into the afterlife is that people here in space time (matter) can no longer hear you. You no longer have a voice with which to make sounds in time and space. It is as described by Fredrick H.W. Myers from the other side:

> *"(I) appear to be standing behind a sheet of frosted glass—which blurs sight and deadens sound".. "A terrible feeling of impotence burdens me."*
>
> (Fredric W. H. Meyers, deceased January 17, 1901, said this speaking back from the other side in 1907).

Next, in the Buddhist death process, inhalation weakens and smell disappears. Individuating wisdom, the energy of desire fades as all notions dim out from your mind. You now feel surrounded by fire flies, sparks, or bursts of light. In my personal experience of returning to the body this sequence was reversed with the fire flies and sparks occurring as I re-entered the body. It was a definite feeling of flames and fire, but not being burned by it because at that moment I had no physical body to feel pain. Yet, I seemed to be enveloped in hundreds of small candle flames or sparklers while re-entering the flesh. (*Hellenistic Mystery religions describe this phenomenon as the baptism of fire which accompanies mystic enlightenment*).

At this point breathing stops and your energy circulation withdraws into the central nervous system. The energy of competitiveness dissipates, tastes are forgotten. The entire body sense fades out and as you depart the flesh you may feel completely enveloped in those small candle flames in your last moments, as your spirit separates from the flesh *(4,500 years ago Thoth-Hermes reportedly said our souls are enveloped in fire)*, and this is my exact remembrance of this experience. Here is what P.H.M. Atwater remembers of this:

> *"Your body goes limp. Your heart stops. No more air flows in or out. You lose sight, feeling, and movement—although the ability to hear goes last.... Identity ceases. The "you" that you once were becomes only memory"..... There is no pain at the moment of death.... Only peaceful silence.... calm..... quiet... But, you still exist........It is easy not to breathe. In fact it is easier, more comfortable, and infinitely more natural not to breathe than to breathe......The biggest surprise for most people in dying is to realize that dying does not end life....... Whatever comes next.... The biggest surprise of all is to realize you are still you. You can still think, you can still remember, you can still see, hear, move, reason, wonder, feel, question, and tell jokes—if you wish.... If you expected to die when you die you will be disappointed. The only thing dying does is help you release, slough off and discard the "jacket" you once wore (more commonly referred to as a "body").....When you die you lose your body. That is all there is to it. Nothing else is lost. You are not your body, It is just something you wear for a while, because living in the earth plane is infinitely more meaningful and more involved if you are encased in its trappings and subject to its rules."[94]*

P.H.M. Atwater

CLINICAL DEATH: This is where you will probably be pronounced clinically dead. But, many Near-Death survivors have gone well beyond this point and then returned again to the former life. For many, to hear their doctor pronouncing them dead, is most distressing. It usually occurs just at the most intense point of physical distress, heart stopping or cessation of breathing.

Yet, at this same point many people describe extremely pleasant feelings and sensations of peace and tranquility. Others report that they experienced various auditory sensations. In some cases there is a loud buzzing noise coming, "from inside my head", or a loud ringing noise, others hear a mighty rushing wind, as did St. Paul during his Near-Death experience with the light on the road to Damascus.

In the Buddhist tradition, what is going on during the pleasant sensations is that the male essence or WHITE awareness now drops like liquid from the brain, descends down the central channel of the chakras to the heart, and you inwardly perceive within the minds "third eye" a sky full of WHITE moonlight. This is what I saw, although I did not associate it with a liquid. Next according to the Buddhist tradition the RED awareness drop, a liquid, which arises as the spirit of enlightenment from the genital wheel toward the heart complex representing the female essence now covers the vision of the third eye with Red.

Personally, without ever reading the *Tibetan Book of the Dead,* I described this same color sequence in reverse, during my return to the body at the close of the NDE. And, I described this RED essence as being the pain of this existence, the feelings within this veil of tears. It was definitely liquid and definitely red to purple and represented the feelings of this life. Jungian psychologists would call it the "Anima" the female feelings essence of physical existence. During my reverse journey this RED liquid blotted out the sky of GOLDEN-ORANGE light. The "liquid" as I observed it, did not necessarily flow "down" although it definitely appeared to flow over my vision. The Buddhist tradition says it flows up from the genitals to the heart. And they also say that to re-enter this life we go through the stages in reverse. My vision of these reverse stages is uncannily parallel to the Buddhist tradition.

LIFTING THE VEIL OF ISIS: The Buddhists stages of the death process describe this going in with this RED bringing on the GOLDEN-ORANGE sunlight. Then proceeding onward into the seventh dissolution called the stage of imminence, at which point the two drops of male (animus) and female (anima) essences meet at the heart. In the physical life these two halves have been separate. Here they enclose the consciousness and you perceive at this point the sky full of bright dark-light, or pure darkness, and then you lose consciousness of this time-space reality (the illusion) as you enter the only true reality of the afterlife. Finally, you pass from this darkness into the realm of clear light translucency (the true reality), gaining an unaccustomed kind of non-dualistic consciousness.

For many people concurrent with the "noise" or a mighty rushing wind they have the sensation of being pulled through a dark tunnel. Most NDE survivors say, we passed through the darkness and then, "we arrived with the light". Western traditions often describe this as a dark tunnel, with the *Light at the end of the tunnel*. New-agers think this "tunnel" is a "worm hole". But, the singular image which I personally find most accurate is the '**Lifting of the veil of Isis**", the point at which this, "Veil of tears" (our earthly life) is forever gone. At which point for me, time and space ceased to operate. The polarization ceases to be in effect, male-female, positive-negative, all "forces" of separation which creates the $E=MC^2$ of our familiar 3-D simply cease. You now pass out of the quantum mechanics matter into the quantum hologram (zero point field) of pure thought. You are now solely the most subtle essence that your consciousness can occupy. Outside of space-time you have no weight, literally no matter. I remember this well. No pain, no time, no space, just the *peace which passes all human understanding*.

OUT OF BODY: Next according to the Buddhist tradition, our extremely subtle consciousness flies out of its location, driven by our evolutionary orientation. According to the Buddhist tradition this is the REAL MOMENT OF DEATH, the Buddhists call it the death-point between. It is the subtlest state possible for a sentient being. It is a state so transparent that anyone unprepared for it will see right through it and not even notice it. This is the Ghost essence, which many researchers are attempting to photograph at known "haunted" locations. One of the earliest recordings of this in Western literature is in Book X of Plato's Republic, where the Greek Soldier Er, reported during a Near-Death experience, that his soul went "out-of-body". And Saint Paul in 2 Corinthians 16 uses the term "out-of-body". This is the point at which your ghost essence has now left the body behind.

Near-Death research has cataloged that your crystal essence, or "spiritual body" takes leave of the flesh shedding the cadaver like a husk or an old snake skin. This is very liberating, because you are no longer confined to matter, but for many souls it is also confusing. Most NDE survivors found themselves floating near the ceiling of the room. At this point you notice that family members, doctors and attendants are still paying attention to your discarded cadaver. You have the definite urge to speak out saying, "Hey, I'm up here, and I'm O.K.". But, of course, without their having studied the death process, they don't know to look for you "up there". You, on the other hand, will be able to see and perceive better than you ever could in the physical life. Indeed, Near-Death survivors who are blind in this physical life, report that when they were on that side of the veil and out-of-body they were able to see quite well.

Descriptions of this "new body" are very difficult for NDE survivors to put into words, however, their descriptions of the properties of the body are decidedly in agreement as follows:

1. Although you may try to communicate with the doctors or relatives in the room THEY CAN'T HEAR YOU.

2. Shortly you also discover that THEY CAN'T SEE YOU. Instead they keep looking at your physical body or cadaver, mistakenly thinking that it is you.

3. You shortly discover that you are weightless You lack a sense of movement, weight, or position. Some people report that they "seemed to be" near the ceiling.

4. Travel is extremely easy, you just think of it and go there. You may shortly discover that you can go through walls and doors.

5. Most people remember their spiritual body as globular or round. Or a mist or smoke like transparent vapor.

6. This out-of-body state is also "timeless". Time has ceased, although events still seem to take place sequentially. If you remain near people trapped in time you can observe their time occurring but you are viewing them from outside of time as if you can look into the future and the past simultaneously.

7. Thoughts and cognition speed up, you can think lucidly and rapidly without making any mistakes. You are literally operating at a higher vibration frequency.

8. Your sense of vision is intact and excellent. People who are blind when alive, report that they regain their vision during the Near-Death experience. Many report that there is no limit to your vision you can look anywhere and everywhere at once.

9. Hearing is changed slightly. Instead of hearing words and sounds you accurately pick up thoughts of people around you (both the living and the dead relatives who have come to greet you). You receive

what they meant, rather than what they said. And, you receive it whether or not they speak it.

Here is how P.H.M. Atwater described this state:

"You are still alive, very much alive. In fact, more alive than since you were last born. Only the way of all this is different, different because you no longer wear a dense body to filter and amplify the various sensations you had once regarded as the only valid indicators of what constitutes life. You had always been taught that one has to wear a body to live."[95] P.H.M. Atwater

At this point, truly intuitive relatives, who are still living and in attendance at your bedside, often realize that you are still there and haven't left after the physical death of your cadaver. Most often these will be women, whose sensitive side has the gnosis that your soul has survived somewhere nearby. They may continue to speak with you for decades. Unfortunately, in our materialistic western science we are taught that speaking to the deceased is a bit crazy. So, this is discouraged in our western culture. But, the truth, which you will encounter when you get to the other side, is that as a disembodied consciousness you can still hear your loved ones. They just can't hear you. If you will find ways to subtly communicate back to them it will reinforce their gnosis that your spirit survives somewhere.

During some NDE's at this point the medical personnel, mistakenly believing they are "helping" you by preventing physical death, courageously start to interfere. Driven by their personal perception of *saving* you, they call for a defilibrator to attempt resuscitation of your cadaver. They take these "heroic" measures honestly believing they are "helping" you. Their training and entire medical MO never considers the possibility that they may be merely meddling and interfering with the timely transition of your on-going consciousness. The truth is that their heroic efforts may be sentencing you to a longer imprisonment in your former body, which may also now be injured and crippled. Keeping you here to live in a crippled body is not at all "saving" you. Indeed, many Near-Death survivors who were enjoying being liberated from the confines of the physical body, have been resuscitated this way by physicians and EMT's. Afterwards, many of these NDE survivors are angry with having been brought back to this prior life *against their will*. They feel truly violated. It is honestly *so good* on the other side that these folks wish they had been allowed to stay dead and to remain over there. This earthly life confined in a body simply does not at all compare with life after death.

Today, there are several documented cases of Near-Death survivors, who have been clinically dead for more than three days, who have then returned to the former body and come back to life. Er was reported to have come back to life 12 days after the battle in which he was killed. So where then is that actual death point?

Unfortunately, many people at this point become quite lonely, realizing that they are going to continue to exist, but that they can't communicate with their relatives who are still living. And if their deceased relatives haven't yet shown up to comfort them they may want to return to physical matter in whatever way presents itself.

DECEASED RELATIVES: Luckily, this is also the point at which many Near-Death survivors report meeting deceased relatives or friends, or in some cases entities (i.e. guardian spirits or masters) who were there to guide, assist and comfort them, and began welcoming them home.

> *"You don't die when you die. You shift your consciousness and speed of vibration. That is all death is...a shift"*[96] P.H.M. Atwater

The Buddhist tradition says that many souls are so unaccustomed to the "liberated" state of the between (or bardo), that they fearfully seek to come back into matter (space-time) as soon as possible and in whatever way possible. The Gnostic Christians described us as being "intoxicated" with matter, as if our spirit is inebriated in its association with matter and that our souls are addicted to having physical form and a body. But, being spirits our true freedom or liberation is to be out of the prison of the body and outside the realm of $E=MC^2$.and the denseness of matter.

THE BEING OF LIGHT: The most profound element in the dying process is the encounter with the Being of Light. Raymond Moody, M.D. interviewed over 150 Near-Death survivors, and provided the following synopsis description of the Being of Light, in his 1975 book *Life after Life*[97]:

> *"Despite the light's unusual manifestations, however, not one person has expressed any doubt whatsoever that it was a being, a being of light. Not only that, it is a personal being. It has a very definite personality. The Love and the warmth which emanate from this being to the*

dying person are utterly beyond words, and he feels completely surrounded by it and taken up in it, completely at ease and accepted in the presence of this being. He senses an irresistible magnetic attraction to this light. He is ineluctably drawn to it.

Interestingly, while the above description of the being of light is utterly invariable, the identification of the being varies from individual to individual and seems to be largely a function of the religious background, or beliefs of the person involved."

In my own personal experience of this *Being of Light*, although I was brought up as a Christian, I also noticed being drawn in and loved beyond words, and I noted it in my journal (five years before publication of Dr. Moody's book) that this Light being, which I saw as the wisdom of the universe, the Christ mind, or the All in All. did not identify itself as any particular entity (Buddha, Christ, Krishna....etc.).

When you encounter the being of light he/she will be asking you a single question, although it has been reported in many forms. The central question is, **"Are you ready to move on?"** But, it comes across to different individuals in different phrases because it is an ESP thought and not a sentence, so when they later try to write it down they will say it differently. But, never does it arrive with judgment nor condemnation. The *Being of Light* is asking you what you think and feel about it. What is your assessment. Typical memories of the questions wording are expressed by experiencers as:

"Are you prepared to die?
"Are you ready to die?"
"What have you done with your life to show me?"
"What have you done with your life that is sufficient?"
"Is it worth it? "

I seems that the *Being of Light* already knows the answer, but is using it to prompt you into analyzing your life. His emotion is helpful and non-threatening. This question usually prompts the *Life Review process*. In the Egyptian papyrus of the "Weighing of the heart" the being of light is the goddess Maat, who is asking these same questions.

THE LIFE REVIEW:

This is where the flashbacks start. Many people have reported that this review covers their entire life, yet takes place in only a few seconds. Even though it is rapid they still experienced all the emotions of the events. This rapid memory has something to do with the increased cognitive capabilities, which are part of the entire experience.

Some people experienced the life review, but not the *Being of Light.* It seems that the thing being reviewed is the emotional and spiritual growth that occurred during each episode of the life being reviewed. The conclusion being sought is not whether it was good or bad, but whether it was worth it. The question seems to be, "Was it complete? Or "Did you learn all the lessons?"

Apparently, the answer has much to do with whether or not you are ready to, "move on". Since, the majority of the first hand reporting available comes from persons who returned to the former life, in these instances they found, after reviewing the data, that they were not ready to move on, or that they had some unfinished business left to accomplish, and hence their decision to return.

There is some limited first hand reporting of this experience, which comes from past life regressions, where the person recalling the past lives also recalls the time and experiences between lives. These people report the same experience:

> *"We know when we have accomplished what we were sent down here to accomplish. We know when the time is up, and you will accept your death for you know that you can get nothing more out of this lifetime. When you have had the time to rest and re-energize your soul, you are allowed to choose your re-entry back into the physical state......Everybody's path is basically the same. We all must learn certain attitudes while we're in physical state......Some of us are quicker to accept them than others. Charity, hope, faith, love...we must all know these things and know them well. ......The reward is in doing without expecting anything,.. doing unselfishly."*[98]

Brian L. Weiss, M.D.

THE BORDER OR LIMIT: In a few instances Near-Death experiencers have reported that they seemed to be approaching a limit or border beyond which they could not go. But, this is not the majority experience. Considering that all of those reporting this boundary, were people who came back, it seems that this probably represents the point of crossing over, or the point of "no return", to the prior life. This brings up the question of, "Why these people returned and did not move on? And, also the question of, "Why do we come back in later lives?"

> *"One must have patience.....patience and timing.....
> everything comes when it must come. A life cannot be
> rushed, cannot be worked on a schedule as so many peo-
> ple want it to be. We must accept what comes to us at a
> given time, and not ask for more. But, life is endless, so
> we never die; we were never really born. We just pass
> through different phases. There is no end. Humans
> have many dimensions. Time is not as we see time, but
> rather in lessons that are learned."*[99] Brian L. Weiss, M.D.

> *"Those are different levels of learning, and we must
> learn some of them in the flesh. We must feel the pain.
> When you're a spirit you feel no pain. It is a period of
> renewal. Your soul is being renewed. When you're in
> physical state in the flesh, you can feel pain; you can
> hurt. In spiritual form you do not feel. There is only
> happiness, a sense of well-being, But it's a renewal
> period for... us. The interaction between people in the
> spiritual form is different. When you are in physical
> state.... You can experience relationships".*[100]
>
> Brian L. Weiss, M.D.

From all of this evidence; my experience, Dr. Brian Weiss' experience, all the NDE survivor's experience, Dr. Stevensen's research on past life memories, PSI and the underlying consciousness in the hidden variables of the state vector collapse in quantum mathematics, two things become clear:

- Life is continuous beyond death, and survival of the individual consciousness is valid.
- Reincarnation is also valid.

CHAPTER 10

THE AFTERLIFE ROAD MAP

WHAT'S NEXT? - Afterlife beyond the Near-Death experience:

WHERE DO WE GO FROM HERE? At this point you have left the physical body and continue to exist as the ghost essence, and what happens next depends on a number of things. Buddhists would say it depends on how prepared you are for this "between" stage (the "bardo" between lives). In my collective research I have identified four possible trip agendas through the undiscovered country which may now take place.

AGENDA 1: ROUND TRIP TICKET: On this temporary excursion, you will shortly decide to come back to life in the old body. This is the trip I took, and nearly all Near-Death survivors remember making the decision to return while they were on the other side, as I did. Or, at least they remember being told by the *Being of Light* that it wasn't their time yet. I remember clearly receiving the message,
"Yet, a little while longer and then you can come home to the Light".

So, if you find out that you are on such a round trip excursion, then you return to this current physical life and like the rest of the NDE survivors, you will have trouble relating about your Near-Death experience, to doctors and clergy, who often refuse to believe you.

Strangely, they have never been there, but even so, they are absolutely convinced that they know better than you do, even though you've been there and they haven't. In their abject ignorance they may arrogantly treat you as if you are slightly crazy. I have had them say ignorant things like, *"What you describe does not agree with scripture...therefore it simply can't be true."* Your relatives may even try to get you to see a shrink. Instead, it will be best for you to join the *International Association for Near Death Studies* (IANDS). There you will find thousands of people who agree with you, because they've made the trip themselves. They know that the unbelieving Doctors and clergy are entirely ignorant and have unknowingly bought into the politically correct agenda of not believing in the survival of the consciousness. However, your joining with other experiencers in IANDS has great therapeutic value because after your return you will spend the remainder of your days in this physical life eagerly anticipating your return to death and the realms of glory which lie just beyond the veil.

> *"If a man dies shall he live again? All the days of my appointed time will I wait, Till my change comes."*
>
> Job 14:14 (NIV)

AGENDA 2: THROUGH TRIP TICKET: This is an excursion where you go on and re-incarnate into a new human life. When you do reincarnate as a small child and later, at the age of three to five years old, begin to speak of your prior life, you will of course, have trouble telling your new parents about your former life. Luckily, by the time you are seven or eight you will tend to forget about the former life.

I like to think of this age as "the age of forgetfulness", as Wordsworth described it.

> *"Not in entire forgetfulness, trailing clouds of Glory we come."*

Your parents in your new life may already be conditioned by their, *one life perspective* here in space-time and themselves being beyond the age of 7 or 8, have now entirely forgotten their own prior lives. So, quite naturally they think they are "older and wiser" than you. They will usually disbelieve, when you describe your former life, especially if they are from a tradition that does not believe in reincarnation.

But, before you reincarnate you will spend some time in the between (the bardo) The Buddhist tradition fears this between time while you are waiting to reincarnate into a new life. They are afraid that you will not be prepared for this between (the bardo), and being fearful of the unknown that you may impetuously take any possible avenue presenting itself for a return to your accustomed state of attachment to matter. The Buddhist's fear that you may, in your haste and not being familiar with the proper path, end up in a new physical body as a sentient being, but not necessarily as a human (maybe in your haste to regain physical matter you come back as a bird or an insect). The key while in the bardo is to learn patience before you get there and not to seek the instantaneous gratification of returning to the flesh.

AGENDA 3: STAY CLOSE TO HOME: This third alternative seems to explain ghost hauntings and photos of ghost essences. In this instance you don't re-incarnate immediately and instead just hang out for a while in the between.

Like, Bonkuch Promisn, the man who was murdered and waited seven years in the tree above the scene of his death, literally hanging out in his ghost essence haunting the site of his trauma. Later, Bonkuck followed a man home who had passed by one day and subsequently, when that man's wife became pregnant Bonkuk's consciousness entered the fetus and he became their son. At the age of three he began telling his new parents about his prior life, and upon investigation researchers verified the prior identity and the killing. As he grew older in the new life he continued to dislike and shun his former killers.

You may haunt some place, especially if you had a traumatic death. This is what many have come to believe is going on with poltergeist type hauntings. The Spiritualist movement believes that people stuck here may not yet know they are dead. This is especially true of traumatic deaths where the spirit may continue to haunt the location of the death for many years like Charlie Crockett.

AGENDA 4: ONE WAY TICKET: This is where you move permanently or at least semi-permanently to that Undiscovered Country, in either of two ways:

    A. It may be as the Buddhists suppose, that there is a fourth choice. We go to commune continuously with the *Being of Light* in literal *Buddha-hood*. At which point we remain an enlightened graduate who is no longer intoxicated with matter and is content to hang out in spirit. I like to think of this Light as the *Christ Mind*, or in hermetic language the *"All"*. When I was there with the light I felt an incredible at-one-ment. Being an integral piece of the Light. I was definitely at home at last. Communing with that enlightened Buddha-hood was fine with me if it lasted for all eternity. Unfortunately my journey had been booked with a round trip ticket and the light shared with me that my consciousness needed to return to earthly life. So I came back, reentered my prior body and "woke up".

B. Or, you may rest with the light for a lengthy sojourn of R & R, before returning to a new life incarnate in a new physical body. How long this R & R lasts is difficult to describe, because it occurs outside time and space, and is therefore ineffable here in space-time.

C. There is also the possibility that as we progress spiritually we move on into further realms or planes of existence (alternate universes), or higher levels. If you find this is true and if I haven't yet made my own final transition, then please communicate back to me about your findings so that I can communicate it to the other readers.

Some people want to know whether we must re-incarnate or can we instead choose to just stay with the light. This is a very good question, the answer for which mankind has been searching for countless millennia. Unfortunately, I was only a tourist there in the undiscovered country, on a fairly low budget whirlwind "round trip" tour. I certainly did not take citizenship classes and become naturalized, so I am not privy to the exact politics of that foreign place. Therefore, I refuse to speculate, unlike, the guru's, imams, priests and pastors who, although they have never been there themselves, seem more than happy to speculate about what they consequently cannot possibly know anything about. Indeed, it is exactly that kind of unfounded speculation from which all the world's religions have created the unfounded *Belief Systems* (BS) that have confounded our world with religious wars. By contrast to such revered fables, I am instead interested only in verifiable facts. Real facts which can only be gleaned by comparing notes with fellow travelers, and by not listening to those who haven't ever been there, but instead want to speculate.

In all seriousness I suggest that to answer this question you can simply remember to ask it next time you are there with *the Light*. And then, if possible, do get back to me with the answer through an after death communication, either through a medium or show up in person as an apparition, or in a new life look me up when you are again old enough to do so.

The fact is well documented among NDE circles that when we are on that side of the veil, there isn't anything that we cannot know if need arises. Over there we are part of *Infinite Intelligence*, plugged into all that is known in the quantum hologram (Akashic record). We are literally fully connected to the *Conscious Universe*, we are part of all knowledge and can access any needed information. But, when we return to this side (physical life), embedded in matter (time and space) we somehow agree to have only limited perspectives and therefore deprive ourselves temporarily of being the all knowing.

CHAPTER 11

CONTINUING AFTERLIFE

WHAT HAS BEEN LEARNED FROM AFTER DEATH COMMUNICATIONS:
This is an area where it is harder to nail down concrete descriptions of the terrain. Firstly, all of the Near-Death survivors came back on a round trip ticket without crossing over permanently. It is like enrolling in college; they have been to the University campus and talked to the Dean, but they haven't matriculated yet at that school, so they can't report with any authority about what college life is going to be like. Secondly, the information we receive through After-Death communications (ADC), is contradictory.

In earlier times skeptics pointed out those contradictions as evidence that all ADC was a hoax. However, we have now collected sufficient reports from the other side to collate the information and we find that there are many correlations. For instance; people visiting the same vicinity or estate on the other side are reporting similar things. But, not everyone reporting back is visiting the exact same estate in their tour of the other side, so the reports naturally differ.

Think about it, if you had two friends that spend the summer in Europe, one visiting Italy, and one visiting Scotland, they would not be telling you the same story when they called your cell phone. The afterlife is the same way, but, because the religious past of our culture has taught us to believe that everyone visiting the other side will have identical experiences, that is how we unconsciously expect it to be.

Yet, it is really not reasonable to assume that everyone will have identical experiences. This is a subconscious expectation which allows skeptics to disbelieve when the various reports from the other side disagree on the details.

The following is a collation of what has been discovered by those studying ADC. It is presented in the format of answers to the most often asked questions:

QUESTION 1 - "HOW LONG IS THE BETWEEN LIFE BEFORE WE CAN REINCARNATE AND GET BACK TO THE PHYSICAL LIFE?"

This is a prominent question because in this physical life we are "intoxicated" with matter. We are somewhat like a drunk anticipating his next drink. It seems because we only identify the physical as being real that we all are anxious to know, "How long before we can be part of physical matter again and re-enter this great illusion called physical existence?" (i.e. How long before my next fix?) and "When does happy hour start again?"

We should instead be asking the question, "Is there something coming next that is better than this physical reality?

But the short answer to the question of how soon we can reincarnate is, "I don't really know". But, I can tell you that time ceases when you are out of body. So, when you get to the other side there is no such concept there as, "How long". The second thing I can tell you, from my own experience, is that after you get over the initial shock of not having a physical body, you will quickly begin to enjoy being there much more than you enjoy being here. It is truly great, there is no pain, and also no emotion, just "the peace which passes all human understanding". It was frankly the best place I have ever been.

Most Near-Death survivors will agree with that assessment, and they simply did not want to come back to this physical life. But, if you really want to know the answer to that question of how long is the between lives, then would you please see if you can find out the answer the next time you are there with the light and report the answer back to me so I can tell others what you found out. There are two ways to report back, either in person when you reincarnate, or from the other side through a medium.

The next question, which usually comes into reader's minds, is again driven by our familiarity with physical bodies:

QUESTION 2 – WHAT WILL MY SPIRITUAL BODY BE LIKE?"….."WILL IT HAVE HANDS, ARMS AND LEGS?"...."OR, WILL I JUST BE A PIECE OF VAPOR LIKE SMOKE?"

Again this question is motivated by our cultural grounding in physical time and space (intoxication with matter). Before the computer age gave us a different perspective we could not fathom a state of not having physical-mechanical strength. Now, however, since the advent of the Internet we have begun to comprehend what Pierre Teilhard de Chardin calls the noosphere, which defines an existence outside the physical, a strictly mental-informational existence. Yet, this question I can answer definitively, based not only on reports from the other side, but also on the reports of many NDE survivors, the research of the Psychical Societies, and the research of the Tibetan Buddhists as well as my own experience.

Most of the time, in the afterlife you will have a "bubble like" essence, more like an energy center within the quantum hologram Occasionally, it appears that this energy disturbance can be photographed by people on this side using carefully manipulated cameras, however, what they are photographing is not a disincarnate consciousness, but is merely the energy disturbance that this consciousness causes in the physical reality when this energy from the zero point field is present. This disturbance sometimes appears in the photographs as being circular.

When you are out of body and located in this center (ghost essence), which usually hangs out near the ceiling when indoors, you will be able to see and hear everything going on around you both near and far through hyper ESP capabilities. Your essence can pass through doors and walls, because you are pure energy and will not have a physical presence in matter. On the other hand, if you need a, "hand" a non-physical one will appear for you.

There are also differing opinions about all this. For instance, the Spiritualists tend to report that we maintain the same geometric bodies, but that they are just much less dense, where the Buddhists see a more spherical essence.

So, again it would be helpful for those of us left here on the physical plane, if once you arrive in the afterlife you would get back to us with a clearer description of what our bodies are like in that undiscovered country.

QUESTION 3 - CAN I CALL HOME FROM THE OTHER SIDE?

Apparently you can, but the ease with which you can accomplish this is going to be dependent upon how receptive your loved ones left behind here in the physical are toward such forms of communication. You simply can't call someone who refuses to answer the phone. If you need to become visible to a loved one to re-assure them, you can project a holographic apparition of your old self for them, momentarily. Sometimes that will shock them into trying to find a way for you to communicate with them. When you are in the afterlife, you can see and hear your still living loved ones, although, they can not see or hear you. But, they can sense your presence and you can communicate across the divide, especially if they are a sensitive person in touch with their own feelings. Unfortunately, you can only "talk" to them through whatever medium they will allow (dreams, psychic readers, etc.) and they have to be receptive to the idea that you may communicate and also take some initiative. If they finally want to communicate with you they may attend circles (séances) with mediums who can establish the necessary p-car resonance with you for them.

Unfortunately, since most people do not consult regularly with mediums, or the tarot, the sad truth is that your loved ones will probably not even try to communicate ever. Consequently, these avenues may be indefinitely closed to you, in which cast you will probably be able to talk through a medium to the folks in attendance, but if your loved ones or one of their friends are not in attendance then you won't get to talk to them. Lastly you can consider visiting their dreams.

On the other hand, once you are on the other side, it is so peaceful there that you won't miss your still living relatives and you haven't got any news to tell them about the afterlife which they won't learn on their own when they die. Actually, since you leave feelings and emotions with the physical body, You will most likely only be moved to communicate back to them thoughts of, "*Not to worry and that you are O.K.*" And, always if they invoke your attention, you will easily come to listen, coming from ..."Near.... Far.... or wherever you are".

Monty Keen (deceased 2004) left his wife Veronica here, but because she is regularly in touch with numerous mediums, he communicated with her often and even said that he was excited about how easy it was to stay in touch. Fredric Myers (deceased 1901),

found it difficult to keep in touch, but the woman he was most intimate with had also preceded him in death, so he was doing most of
his after death communications on the scientific level with the SPR,
and not on the personal level.

My personal opinion is that communicating from the other side
with a loved one should be easier than Myers trying to communicate
with a mere business acquaintance.

Further, when you are over there, you know that when your relatives
finally enter the afterlife you will be there to greet them, and since
time has ceased on that side of the veil, for you it is only a little while
until you will be greeting them on their arrival in the afterlife. So
there is little anxiety on your part about communicating back to
those who will join you shortly. Also, you know that no matter what
they believe about the afterlife, they are going to find out the truth
when you greet them. So, consequently, there is no rush or anxiety
about communicating back to them.

QUESTION 4: WHAT IS IT LIKE THERE ON A DAILY BASIS?

Actually, because I was on a round trip ticket, I did not get much
personal knowledge of the day to day existence in the afterlife. So,
I can not tell you for sure. But, I will rely on what Edward C. Randall
reported from his analysis of over 15 years of discussions with disincarnate beings on the other-side aided by medium Emily French.
Karmic laws state that we don't change..... According to Randall's
research the insane pass from physical life into the afterlife and are
still insane,.....good people are still good, and the bad ones are still
bad.

But, there is a great difference. On the other side some individuals
may work in mental health services helping those who are insane to
regain their minds. Also many children who were not born physi-
cally into this life, come to the afterlife and it is reported by Edward
C. Randall that many women who never knew motherhood in physical life (but wanted children) are allowed in the afterlife to work at
taking care of these children and satisfy any craving they had for
motherhood in a win-win situation.

Randall, also reports that murderers at war with humanity in the
physical life are redirected when they get to the afterlife into the
karma of love and goodness. Death does not change people, and
there is just as great a need for schools and colleges in the afterlife

as exists in the physical life. There is no need for money so the main activity of the earthly life (gathering money) is non-existent in the afterlife. It is only by helping others there and those left behind in this physical life that any progress is made by your surviving consciousness.

The law of attraction is the dominate force there. There is no aristocracy there except mind and merit. Want to join a higher level there.....then improve your heart and mind....you can even start now before you die. Here is what Edward C. Randall recorded about this:

> *"One who has given all or nearly all of his time and thought to material things has so much to learn on arriving here* (in the afterlife), *that it is a comparatively long time before he begins to 'find' himself sufficiently to understand and enjoy the spiritual life. Such a one, if he had given more time and thought to spiritual things during his earth life, could immediately have claimed his spiritual treasures – which would have been carefully stored up for him until such time as he had need of them – and would have been helped and his new life* (here in the afterlife) *made much easier and pleasanter by the possession of these riches. As it is, he has to make his way just as a penniless wayfarer, on arriving in a new locality, must set about earning his daily bread in the material world."*

> A consciousness speaking from the afterlife to Randall in 1906

QUESTION 5: ARE THERE LEVELS IN THE AFTERLIFE?

Saint Paul says when describing his Near-Death experience in Second Corinthians 12 that he was lifted up to *the third heaven.* French & Randall report that there are several spheres. Some Buddhists & Hindus believe that these spheres are similar to our Chakras, or in the Kaballah they are the levels in the Tree of Life.

Unfortunately, because the dimensions of space are not conceptual restrictions in those energy fields where the afterlife resides this is a tough question to answer. Many NDE survivors have tried to explain what they experienced about "levels", but, their descriptions appear to disagree quantitatively but not qualitatively. Consequently, I do believe there are stages of development over there, but I don't believe anybody has valid clues as to how they might be formed or what meanings they might have. Even if we knew what the intent of these levels was, it is probably a concept which is ineffable in our space-time based language. Suffice it to say that everyone reports levels or stages of progress in the afterlife. And nearly all see it as the next chapter in the same on-going progress of our consciousness.

DIFFICULTIES TO BE CONSIDERED:

The following impressions of the other side are my own opinion based on my own experiences and extensive research:

1. Intellect operates at maximum capability because it is no longer distracted by the noise of feeling and emotion, which stayed behind with the physical body.

2. A disincarnate consciousness experiences minimal feelings, the only feelings are intellectual or "remembered" feelings. If they had strong relationships when here in the physical life, then they remember these. However, they are apparently not moved by any passions.

3. Intellectual / spiritual advancement is stunted, because without feelings (which are based in physical tissues) emotional learning can not advance. While over on the other side with our expanded intellect, we can analyze lessons remembered from the prior physical life, and use our better intellect to think critically and thus advance our viewpoint before reincarnating in to a new physical body. Yet, all *emotional* learning is stunted there and must be accomplished in physical life. Dr. Brian Weiss reports one "Master" who has reincarnated 86 times.

4. Communication from the afterlife to the earth plane is complicated for several reasons:
   A. NUANCES OF SPECIFIC LANGUAGE ARE LOST: All after death communications, other than electronic voice or direct voice phenomena, must be delivered to you through symbols (i.e. visions in a medium's mind, or dreams in the minds of your still living loved ones).
   B. LOST IN TRANSLATION: It must often be delivered through mediums who may not have the background for the material being transmitted. (i.e. they see the correct symbols but don't have the personal experience to know

what those symbols mean to you or your loved ones), e.g. they lack the technical jargon required for your specific message.

C. THE LISTENER IS NOT LISTENING: Loved ones on the earth plane may not believe that the disincarnate consciousness of their departed loved one is trying to communicate. Most living persons are not involved with the Spiritualist movement, and do not attend circles where it would be possible for their departed loved one to contact them through a medium for two-way conversation.

D. ONE SIDED CONVERSATIONS: Because those on this side generally are not listening for an ADC, most communication is forced to be one-way and subliminal, more like an advertising billboard which the recipient may not notice.

5. Unfortunately, not everyone believes in ADC but they should. A body is said to possess energy when it is capable of producing an effect and it requires some level of energy to communicate. Apparitions and other communications effects like tarot, automatic writing, speaking through mediums, are evidence of energy transmission, and even though these may be subtle energy levels, they do consume some form of energy. The fact that these communications are received at all indicates that some agency is expending the energy to transmit them. Consequently, if the communication is at all coherent and intelligible, and not merely static, then it is clear evidence that there is a living consciousness on the other side generating that message, i.e. when a message is received it should be a clear indication that a surviving intellect sent it.

LAND OF MYSTERY: Knowing exactly what that undiscovered country is like while contemplating the shadowy and disconnected reports coming back from explorers who have preceded us will remain difficult at best. The afterlife is like a newly discovered planet, and we are receiving seemingly conflicting reports about a very real place.

For example, NASA has been looking for signs of life on planet Mars, yet the current exploratory probes are showing differing results. Several years ago our probes found only rock, but the Phoenix in 2008 finds ice (water) as soon as it lands, just under a surface covering of dust. This latest report changes most of what we thought we knew from the prior probes. Until this probe landed, the *believed wisdom* was that there was no water on Mars, because "canals on mars" had been disproved generations ago. But, since 2008 everyone knows there was once liquid water on Mars and there is much frozen water on Mars at the moment.

Similarly, with the reports coming in from Near-Death survivors there have been differing descriptions of the landscape discovered. But, what is so compelling about NDE reports is how similarly all of them describe the journey itself (i.e the traveling out-of-body and the stages of the transition). Over 2500 years of recorded NDE reports there is nothing new regarding the process of getting to the afterlife. The process as documented today by IANDS is still, as it always was described by the Hindus, Buddhists. Platonists, neo-Platonists, St. Paul and the early Christian church (as clearly stated in the systematic theology of Origen). It is only since Justinian's adoption of the single life theory along with the ego-centric materialist paradigm that we have lost sight of this truth.

For a further in depth discussion of the eastern (Hindu) interpretation of similar afterlife material see Deepak Chopra's 2007 book *Life After Death: The Burden of Proof* which describes how the afterlife may be according to various eastern traditions.

CHAPTER 12

WHAT ALL THIS MEANS

"We now have, for the first time in the history of our species, compelling empirical evidence for belief in some form of personal survival after death."
1993, Robert Almeder, PhD. Professor of Philosophy, Georgia
State University

No creature has meaning without the Word of God.
God's Word is in all creation, visible and invisible.
The Word is living, being, spirit, all verdant greening,
all creativity
This Word flashes out in every creature.
This is how the spirit is in the flesh – the Word is
indivisible from God.[101]

Hildegard of Bingen
(1098-1179 AD)

Every soul...... comes into this world strengthened by the victories or weakened by the defeats of its previous life. Its place in this world as a vessel appointed to honor or dishonor is determined by its previous merits or demerits. Its work in this world determines its place in the world which is to follow this one.[102]

Origen, Alexandrian Christian circa 210 AD, De Principis

"Just take time *out of it and then it all makes sense"*[103]
Robert Jahn, Former Dean of Engineering Princeton

"What we have been doing... is laying the foundation for a religion of the 21st century"[104]

Evan Harris Walker, PhD. Physics

POSITIVE SCIENTIFIC PROOF:

It is clear that consciousness survival and the afterlife can be demonstrated well enough to provide the *preponderance of evidence* required for proof in court. However, science has always held proof of any hypothesis to a higher level known as *proof by replication:*

PROOF BY REPLICATION: What science requires for valid replication when working in the realm of our space-time reality is a standardized experiment which can be set up by any scientist using identical apparatus and after following the same series of steps finds the same results.

Unfortunately, this system of proof assumes that the replicating scientists will have the same powers of objective observation which were possessed by the original experimenter. The Heisenberg principle of uncertainty expressed as the observer phenomena, shows that neither the original scientist nor the one trying to replicate the experiment are in actuality objective observers, but instead that both consciously effect the results of their experiment.

Also, when portions of the experiment to be replicated actually operate outside of space-time, then part of the apparatus required to make the observations may in fact be psychic capability. If the replicating scientist lacks these specialized faculties which the original experimenter may have possessed, then the experiment simply cannot be replicated by the second scientist with weak or completely undeveloped psychic powers.

The experimenter's consciousness participates in the experiment and affects the results. In other words, "You find what you are looking for". Consequently, a skeptical scientist with a materialistic mind set who has no belief in things not physical, and hence who therefore also has no psychic ability will find when he/she attempts to replicate these experiments that they will automatically fail. This then makes replication, for most materialist minded scientists, patently impossible.

REPLICATION BY CORRELATION:
Therefore, when we work outside the box of this space-time reality, we cannot necessarily follow the 19th century rules of proof which were developed entirely inside the box of Newtonian materialism. Instead, we need to use totally different criteria to define replication

and proof. Consequently, I propose a new form of scientific replication by correlation:

- Realizing that the goal of replication is to
  achieve the same results,
- Also noting that we are working, in this specific
  instance, with results which cannot be objectively observed in space-time reality, simply
  because they do not take place there.
- On the other hand, if the same results can be
  arrived at from different avenues each of which
  is pursued independently, then should that not
  be sufficient replication to establish the truth of
  the identical results as being factual.

We can easily find this level of replication in the nearly identical
descriptions of the death process which come to us from the following four separate and independent fields of endeavor, but all
arriving at the same conclusion about the death process:

1. THE NEAR DEATH EXPERIENCE:

We have discussed at length the Near-Death experience and the
description of the death process which this field of inquiry repeatedly records. After careful analysis of thousands of Near-Death narratives we have developed a fairly standard sequence for the death
process. This provides sufficient replication to verify that the NDE is
indeed factual. I have studied and worked with this technical
description for over 30 years, and these thousands of NDE narratives replicate my own experience from 1970. But, their replication
of my experience only proves that the Near-Death experience itself
is what everybody experiences WHEN THEY RETURN TO THIS
LIFE AFTER ALMOST DYING which is why we call it the "Near-
Death" experience, rather than an "Experience of Death", we know
for sure that they "nearly died" but even though they may have been
declared dead, with all bodily functions having ceased, we still can't
prove that this is the same process they would experience if they did
not return to this life and had instead remained dead.

On the other hand, the following are incidents of replication of the
Near-Death experience, coming from other areas of scientific inquiry
which validate the fact that the NDE is the same process which occurs
when the patient stays dead and moves on to the afterlife.

2. AFTERLIFE COMMUNICATIONS:

In 1906, nearly 65 years before I had my NDE, Edward C. Randall, a prominent New York Lawyer, published a description of the dying process. (see chapter 5) He had received this description through After-Death communications (ADC) with a surviving consciousness, on the other side, That surviving consciousness identified himself as being the late Dr. David C. Hossack, who had died some 60 years prior to his communications with Randall. My research into Dr. Hossack's identity has found that he was a former professor at Columbia University (King's College), and the founder of the Columbia Medical School, who had graduated from Princeton and then received his medical degree in Philadelphia in 1791, and later studied abroad at Edinburgh, Scotland before returning to New York to teach at King's College (Columbia University). Dr. Hossack was also one of the founders of the New York Historical Society in 1804, and he personally established the Elgin Botanical Garden between 47th and 51st streets and 5th and 6th Avenues. Dr. Hossack died around 1840.

Edward C. Randall himself had never had a Near-Death experience and lived in an age when this was not yet a known medical phenomenon. In his writing he never mentions anything like and NDE or someone returning from the dead. Also, at the time when Randall wrote; Plato's descriptions and St. Augustine's descriptions of the NDE, as well as the Tibetan Book of the dead, were still very obscure and unknown in the West. The Egyptian Book of the Dead had not yet been fully translated, although some parts had appeared in German translation as early as 1842. Consequently, it is highly unlikely that Randall could ever have heard of anything like an NDE. Yet, Randall's description of the dying process is identical to what occurs in all modern NDE's. Randall states that this death process was described to him by the surviving consciousness of Dr. Hossack through the phenomena of direct voice surrounding the medium Mrs. French

The fact that the death process Randall reported in 1906 matches what I myself experienced in 1970 is, to me, rather compelling proof that Randall did get this information from a surviving consciousness who had been through the same experience that I had, but remained dead. Also, because the description agrees so closely with what is experienced in the modern NDE, it is apparent that his account could not have been creative fiction. If Randall had made it up he would have gotten some of the details differently.

Indeed, the only real difference between my experience and Dr. Hossack's is that I returned to the prior life and Dr. Hossack went on into the afterlife. Consequently, Randall's account provides very strong replication showing that the death process is identical to the Near-Death process.

3. TIBETAN BOOK OF THE DEAD:

Finally, in my research I studied the description of the death process in the Tibetan Book of the Dead, and found that it correlates very nearly with my own experience as well as the experience described by Randall. Yet, this Tibetan description was from over 800 years ago and thus provides a second replication from an alternate source. The Tibetan book is describing either a recorded Near-Death process or an actual death process as received by After-Death communication, but since it agrees with both my own experience and Dr. Hossack's it again shows that the actual death process is identical to the Near-Death process.

4. MEMORIES OF PAST LIVES:

Several people who remember past lives, as reported by Ian Stevenson at the University of Virginia, have also related their experience of the time spent between lives while living as an out-of-body consciousness, which provides a third replication from an alternate source, which again shows that the actual death process is identical to the Near-Death process.

Consequently, in my opinion, these four matching accounts are sufficient replication to prove scientifically that the Near-Death experience is identical to what happens when each of us finally dies.

SUMMATION: Here is what these cross-corresponding replications also prove to be fact:
1. **NEAR-DEATH EXPERIENCES ARE REAL:** For over 2500 years people have been recording reports of Near-Death experiences where they traveled out of body to an afterlife. An alternative reality located in another dimension, or plane of existence just beyond our physical reality, on the other side of the veil.
2. **MEMORIES OF PAST LIVES ARE REAL:** Over the last 50 years, thousands of children have been reporting past lives which have been scientifically documented and verified.

3. **AFTERDEATH COMMUNICATIONS ARE REAL:** For over 150 years, mediums and everyday folks have been receiving After-Death Communications from the surviving consciousness of friends and relatives still living somewhere in an afterlife, which takes place in a different, but parallel dimension.

4. **THE NEW PHYSICS SUPPORTS ALL OF THIS:** Non-locality, quantum mathematics and the quantum hologram provide a scientific basis for all of these phenomena to properly exist within the laws of physics. So it is no longer considered impossible for the disembodied consciousness to occupy an alternative reality in as yet undiscerned dimensions (afterlife).

5. **THIS AGREES WITH THE CHRISTIANITY OF THE EARLY CHURCH:** The words of Jesus, St. Paul and the early Christian fathers (Gregory of Nyssa, Origen of Alexandria, Jerome) support all of this. I will be covering this in detail in later books.

6. **THERE IS NO SCIENTIFIC EVIDENCE TO CONTRADICT ANY OF THE ABOVE:** While there is a preponderance of empirical and anecdotal evidence supporting universal survival of the consciousness in an afterlife, there is on the other hand absolutely no contrary evidence, which has ever been presented to refute consciousness survival.

7. Unfortunately, conflicting religious beliefs, dogmas and taboos have clouded our understanding of all this.

8. Further complicating the issue is the ontology of materialist scientists who refuse to accept the realities of quantum mechanics and still persist in holding the Cartesian perspective of a Newtonian mechanistic universe. Their tunnel vision hinders widespread understanding of these new concepts

Here is how a leading Psychiatrist sums up these collected facts:
I believe that each of us possesses a soul that exists after the death of the physical body and that it returns time and time again to other bodies.....There is no empirical evidence for this...But, the anecdotal evidence is overwhelming and to me unassailably conclusive......I no longer doubt that reincarnation is real. Our souls have

ng__ __

> *lived before and will live again, That is our immortal-*
> *ity......I see the soul as a body of energy that blends*
> *with universal energy, then splits off again, intact, when*
> *it returns to a new life......We are immortal..... We are*
> *eternal.... Our souls will never die...his being so, we*
> *should start acting as if we know immortality is our*
> *blessing*[105]

Brian L. Weiss, M.D. 2003 AD

This collected evidence agrees with modern physics and quantum mechanics, and also collates with the original religion of ancient Egypt (Perennial Philosophy[106]) as well as early Christianity. Further, since the late 1970's all of this has become the new frontier of cutting edge science as described by one quantum physicist:

> *"Everything we know about Nature is in accord with the idea*
> *that the fundamental process of Nature lies outside space and*
> *time........ But generates events that can be located in space-*
> *time".*[107]

Henry Stapp quantum physicist U. Cal.

To paraphrase Stapp,

> *The Conscious Universe which exists outside of our three*
> *dimensions of space-time, is the fundamental non-local force*
> *which allows the generation of everything that is located here in*
> *space - time.*

> *The Zero Point Field (ZPF) provides the energy which is pro-*
> *jected holographically from the additional dimensions of dark*
> *energy (postulated by string theory and M-theory) that is*
> *instantaneously transformed (by consciousness generating the*
> *state vector collapse) into what we continually experience as the*
> *physical reality (matter) here in space-time.*

QUANTUM RESONANCE:

We tend to perceive science as being the ultimate truth, but it is really only a series of short stories collected into a larger anthology. We grew up with the idea that if we could learn all the disconnected short stories of science we would be able to discern the "big picture". And part of that big picture was the supporting fiction which told us that our consciousness was just an outgrowth of the physical reality, and that thoughts were just chemical reactions taking place in the synapses of a "wet" computer called our brain, which itself was just the natural result after billions of years of Darwinian evolution.

Unfortunately, we are now approaching a time when such 19th century mechanistic children's fables which we have been spoon fed (as if they were proven scientific truths) are suddenly about to be replaced with a drastically revised version of the "big picture", and the new perspective is one that sees consciousness as the underlying basis of our physical reality. Consciousness (mind) is the basic building block of everything, rather than being an accidental outgrowth of physical matter.

In-other-words, mind is not a by-product of the brain, but instead,
"The brain is only a receiver which the universal mind developed through evolutionary intention, in order to use it as a search engine to establish p-car resonance with the Akashic Field from which to intuit information."

Quantum mechanics has demonstrated to the leading scientific minds that *our entire three dimensional reality is produced by a quantum web of interconnected information transfer which is constantly occurring between living organisms and their surrounding environment.* Other scientists have produced compelling evidence suggesting that **consciousness itself is a substance existing outside the confines of the body.**

Further, it appears that DNA and the neurological system, which were previously thought to be the information conductors of the body, are instead transducers that merely pick up the necessary information from the surrounding quantum hologram.

Finally, even our understanding of the arrow of time, as flowing only in one direction, is now being challenged in leading scientific circles as being merely an incomplete mental construct. This obsolete understanding now needs to be radically revised, in order to suit the observed phenomena, especially in the light of consciousness and the observer role in the state vector collapse.

THE GREAT SHIFT

The Kalachakra Tantra made a prophesy 12 centuries ago, in the 8th century AD which foretold a great shift which would occur in the world's spirituality. Carter Phipps, one of the senior editors at *What is Enlightenment magazine (Now EnlightenNext)*, described this rapidly occurring shift in the current world situation quite poignantly when he said:

> *"Never before in the history of knowledge has there been such a wealth of cross-cultural, cross-disciplinary data converging from so many different streams of experience, all of which is providing hints of what lies beyond the physical veil.....*
>
> *"All of it is contributing to a potential new science of survival re-birth and the non-physical dimensions of existence.....*
>
> *"Indeed we live in an age of discovery, and the veil between this world and whatever lies beyond seems to be yielding its secrets as never before to the endless curiosity of the human mind. And like explorers setting foot on a new continent that was once only the subject of rumor, belief, and speculation, we are establishing beachheads on the subtle sands of the nonphysical realms and getting a sense of the initial landscape."*
>
> Carter Phipps, *What Is Enlightenment*
> Issue 32 March-May 2006

LOGICAL CONCLUSION: All of this evidence points to the fact that the afterlife is no longer a myth of speculation, or a mere hope of salvation. Instead, consciousness survival in an afterlife, outside of our present understanding of the limited 3-D which we can measure, should now be understood as a *proven reality* which is merely the next chapter in the ongoing saga of the journey of our individual consciousness. It should also be clear that we know very little about the afterlife from a factual standpoint and also only very little from a philosophical standpoint. So, we need to research many questions, for instance:

1. What energy form does the consciousness survive in? is it magnetic, electrical, or some as yet undiscovered form of energy existing within the dark energy?

2. How does the spiritual body exist in the afterlife, as a vapor? a bubble? What exactly is the form of this subtle essence?

3. How does the consciousness later re-enter a new physical body, and when does the consciousness enter that new physical body, at birth or, at conception, or is this re-entry random?

4. Does the consciousness advance through various lives, like the various grades of high school and as described in the Hindu belief system?

5. Is it possible to regress in this curriculum? For instance coming back in a lesser life next time around? Say a fish or a raccoon, as is postulated by the Buddhist beliefs?

6. Were we first vegetation (plants and flowers) and did we then become insects and then animals and finally reincarnate as humans? Or, is this entirely not so? Do all things have souls? Do the stones and plants have spirits and consciousness?

7. Do we have free will here in the physical life, or is this carnival ride all planned out in advance and we just follow out the plot?

8. The questions can go on and on, but science needs to get seriously involved, stop ignoring the questions and instead get busy solving them.

Actually, we are on the edge of a new frontier, very much like Europe as the renaissance began to flower in the 1470-90's just before Columbus discovered America. At the time Vikings had been to North America and had brought home legends that were making the rounds, but despite those legends of lands to the west across the Atlantic most Europeans simply *knew* that the world was flat and that if ships went west they would tragically fall off the edge of the earth. Even so, a few brave souls decided to venture out into the frontier. In 1492 Columbus would sail west across the Atlantic to the West Indies in the Caribbean Sea, followed in 1497 by Vasco DaGama who would finish sailing south around Africa arriving in India in 1498. Suddenly, the paradigm shifted and everyone *knew* the earth was round.

RESOURCES IN CONSCIOUSNESS STUDIES:

TIME FOR SCIENTIFIC AFTERLIFE RESEARCH: What is called for today is a shift in our world view, so that we see the afterlife and reincarnation as probable realities. This will free our minds to eagerly support research in those areas which will bring us answers regarding our relationship to the afterlife. We need to support the efforts of afterlife researchers and respect them as the professionals that they are, and also make a conscious decision to believe that their field of study is as important as biology, chemistry, medicine or law.

Much afterlife research is taking place as an adjunct to the expanding field of *Consciousness Research*. This field has gained a large following of intellectuals, physicists, psychiatrists and psychologists who have formed professional organizations to pursue the study of *Consciousness* and the *Afterlife*, and to also publish scientific journals and educational publications in this field. Each of these organizations is very professional and a good source of current and ongoing information in this rapidly expanding and changing field of study

1. Institute of Noetic Sciences (IONS) www.noetic.org
2. International Association for Near-Death Studies (IANDS) www.iands.org
3. Society for Scientific Exploration (SSE) www.scientificexpolration.org
4. EnlightenNext Magazine (WIE): www.wie.org,
5. Society for Psychical Research, (SPR) (Great Britain): www.spr.ad.uk
6. American Society for Psychical Research (ASPR): www.aspr.com
7. Forever Family Foundation www.foreverfamily.org

Check out each of these organizations on line to see what they offer and are doing to further Afterlife Research. Recently the *Forever Family Foundation* was established to allow a forum to publicize the reality of Consciousness Survival, with the following stated purposes:

- To establish the existence of the continuity of the family, even though a member has left the physical world
- To stimulate thought among the curious, those questioning their relationship to the universe, and people who are looking for explanations of certain phenomena
- To financially support the continued research into survival of consciousness and afterlife science
- To provide a forum where individuals and families who have suffered the loss of a loved one can turn for support, information, and hope through state-of-the-art information and services provided by ongoing research into the survival of consciousness and afterlife science.

END NOTES

END NOTES, CHAPTER 1 - INTRODUCTION
[1] *The Varieties of Scientific Experience* by Carl Sagan ©2006, Lecture 1.

END NOTES, CHAPTER 2 – HOW TO USE THIS BOOK
[2] *A Change of Heart: a Memoir,* by Claire Sylvia ©1997

END NOTES, CHAPTER 3 – MY NEAR DEATH EXPERIENCE -
[3] *Gospel of Phillip,* (Nag Hammadi Library Codex II Tractate 3 p.61)

[4] *A Course in Miracles,* Chapter 5, Section VI (1977)

[5] P.39 *Coming Back to Life: The After-Effects of the Near-Death Experience* ©198 P.M.H. Atwater, Balantine Books

[6] St. Paul's letter to the *Ephesians 2:6-9* (NIV)

[7] *Life after Life,* by Raymond L. Moody Jr. M.D. ©1975, 1988 Bantam edition

[8] Ibid.

[9] St. Paul's letter *1 Corinthians 2:4-5* (NIV).

[10] P. 75, *Heading Toward Omega* © 1984, Kenneth Ring

[11] http://www.youtube.com/watch?feature=player_embedded&v=4qUGV4n23dY

[12] *Life After Life* by Raymond A. Moody ©1975. And, a translation by Paul Shorey, in Hamilton and Cairns (ed.), Plato: *The Collected Dialogues* (New York Bollingen Series LXXI, 1961), PP. 838-40

[13] Augustine, St. (2008) *On the care to be had for the dead,* From *the Retractions,* Book ii. Chap. 64. Retrieved from:www.fordham.edu/halsall/source/augustine-onthecare-ofthgedeadnpnf1-03-39.html

END NOTES, CHAPTER 4 - MEMORIES OF PAST LIVES
[14] Moss, Steven A. Moss, "Ecclesiastes 1:4: A Proof Text For Reincarnation", Jewish Bible Quarterly 21.1 (1993) 28-30

[15] *Life After Death* by Bill Newcott p.66 © Sep/Oct 2007, AARP Magazine

[16] Page 140 *Old Souls,* by Tom Schroder ©1999 Simon & Schuster.

[17] Reincarnation, an East-West Anthology, Head and Cranston, ©1967, p. 35-39

[18] Origen, *De Principis*

[19] Reincarnation, an East-West Anthology, Head and Cranston, ©1967, p. 35-39

[20] p.38 *St. Gregory of Nyssa and the rise of Christian mysticism* ©1950 John Trinick: 38

[21] *Twenty Cases Suggestive of Reincarnation*, by Ian Stevensen, M.D ©1974 University of Virginia

[22] *Children Who Remember Previous Lives*, by Ian Stevenson, M.D., ©2001 McFarland & Company, Inc.

[23] *Life Before Life*, by Jim B. Tucker, M.D. ©2995

[24] *Many Lives, Many Masters*, ©1988 by Brian L. Weiss, M.D.

[25] Page 5, *Death and Personal Survival*, by Robert Almeder, ©1992 Rowman & Littlefield Publishers, Inc.

[26] Reincarnation: *Verified Cases of Rebirth After Death*, by K.K.N. Sahay ©1927 N.L. Guipta.

[27] P.183 Immortal Remains: The Evidence for Life After Death, by Stephen E Braude © 2003

[28] P. 183 *Twenty Cases Suggestive of Reincarnation*, by Ian Stevensen, M.D ©1974 University of Virginia.

[29] *Reincarnation in Christianity: A New Vision of the Role of Rebirth in Christian Thought.* ©1978 Geddes MacGregor

[30] Page 19, *Death and Personal Survival*, by Robert Almeder, ©1992 Rowman & Littlefield Publishers, Inc, Almeder also lists numerous other publications which discuss this case uncritically.

[31] Page 68, *Children Who Remember Previous Lives*, by Ian Stevenson, M.D., ©2001 McFarland & Company, Inc.

[32] *Soul Survivor, The Reincarnation of a World War II Fighter Pilot* ©2010 by Bruce & Andrea Leininger.

[33] P. 259 *Twenty Cases Suggestive of Reincarnation*, by Ian Stevensen, M.D ©1974 University of Virginia.

[34] *KOONA: Through the eyes of a Haida Chief* , by Alan Hugenot © 2002 48 Degrees North Magazine – Seattle

While Chief Cumshewa was showing us the ancient village the Chief volunteered a story about a specific reincarnation. This happened spontaneously, although I had never mentioned to him that I had any such interests. Here is how it reads from page 50 of the magazine:

"To be guided through a ghost village, by a Haida elder with the venerable rank of a senior village chief, was an honor not lost on us. Cumshewa handed each of us a book entitled Those Born at Koona, "We'll start on page 14, when we get to the west end of the village", he said softly. We listened attentively , following as he lead us over Koona's sacred grounds, describing the village history in friendly but solemn terms. This was a great man, who was bringing the gift of age and experience to the sharing of his story: the story of both his people and his lifetime.

"The chief, born three decades after Koona was abandoned in 1889, explained that his authority for knowledge of the village came from Jim Jones, whom Cumshewa had fished with, after the second world war. Jim had been born in Koona, and lived here until his teenage years. The Chief showed us Jim's photo in the back of the book, taken at Koona in 1954 when Jim was an old man. The Haida culture teaches that spirits of the deceased return in the *following generations. And Cumshewa shared with us that, "My son Patrick, is a Haida artist, and the Spirit of Jim lives in Patrick, who was born just after Jim died".*

I spoke with Mr. Wesley (Chief Cumshewa) further on this and he told of how Patrick had the same traits as his deceased friend Jim. It was apparent to me from the way Mr. Wesley included these thoughts in everyday conversation that he found it quite normal to believe in reincarnation. Here was a wizened man whom I respected greatly, who believed that our consciousness returns for multiple lifetimes: Now, I was left with a third conviction:

[35] *Those Born at Koona* ©1973 by Carolyn & John Smyly. *This book, used as a reference by Chief Cumshewa, when I was visiting Skedans confirms Jim Jones birth at Koona, and of which I also have a copy.*

[36] *Across Time and Death,* ©1993 Jenny Cockell, Fireside Books, London.

[37] *Someone Else's Yesterday.* ©2003 Jeffrey J. Keene, Blue Doplhin Publishing.

[38] *Jewish Tales of Reincarnation* by Yonassan Gershom ©1999

[39] *Beyond The Ashes: Cases of Reincarnation from the Holocaust,* by Yonassan Gershom ©1992

[40] *From Ashes to Healing: Mystical Encounters wiith the Holocaust,* by Yonassan Gershom ©1996

[41] *Other Lives, Other Selves,* by Roger J. Woolger, PhD© 1988

END NOTES, CHAPTER 5 - AFTER DEATH COMMUNICATIONS

[42] P.170 *Human Personality and Its Survival of Bodily Death,* by F.W.H. Myers ©1903, 1961, 2001

[43] *Life After Death* by Bill Newcott p.66 Sept / Oct 2007 AARP Magazine.

[44] P.87, *The Heart of the Mind* by Jane Katra, PhD. And Russell Targ ©1999, Reuter's News Service January 31, 1998.

[45] P.517-524, *Proceedings: Society for Psychical Research #36,* © 1927, *Parapsychology, A Century of Inquiry,* D.Scott Rogo ©1975

[46] P187, *Ghost Hunters* by Deborah Blum, ©2006, Mediumship & Survival by Alan Gauld ©1983

[47] P275-285, *Ghost Hunters* by Deborah Blum, ©2006

[48] *Natural and Supernatural: a history of the Paranormal,* Brian Inglis ©1977, 1992

[49] P.92, *The Heart of the Mind* by Jane Katra, PhD. And Russell Targ ©1999 The Case of Runolfur Runolfsson P.33-59 Journal of American Society for Pssychical Research No. 69 (1977)

[50] *Survival is in the Details:* Emerging Evidence for Discarnate Intention from Mediumship Research, Gary E Swartz, PhD and Julie Beischel, Phd. ©2006 University of Arizona

[51] Ibid.

[52] P. 201, *Beyond the Ashes,* by Yonassa Gershom ©1992

[53] P. 173, *The French Revelation,* Edward C. Randall's Complete Works Compiled by N. Riley Heagerty ©1995

[54] Dr. David Hossack, Professor at Columbia University (King's College), and founder of the Medical School, graduated from Princeton and received his medical

degree in Philadelphia in 1791, then studied abroad at Edinburgh, Scotland before returning to New York. He was one of the founders of the New York Historical Society in 1804. He also established the Elgin Botanical Garden between 47th and 51st street and between 5th and 6th.

55 Randall   p. 150-151

56 p. 15, *The French Revelation*, Edward C. Randall's Complete Works Compiled by N. Riley Heagerty ©1995

57 p. 148, *The French Revelation*, Edward C. Randall's Complete Works Compiled by N. Riley Heagerty ©1995

58 Dr. David Hossack, Professor at Columbia University (King's College), and founder of the Medical School, graduated from Princeton and received his medical degree in Philadelphia in 1791, then studied abroad at Edinburgh, Scotland before returning to New York. He was one of the founders of the New York Historical Society in 1804. He also established the Elgin Botanical Garden between 47th and 51st street and between 5th and 6th

59 p. 149, *The French Revelation*, Edward C. Randall's Complete Works Compiled by N. Riley Heagerty ©1995

END NOTES , CHAPTER 6 - QUANTUM FIELD THEORY

60 *How to See the Invisible: 3 Approaches to Finding Dark Matter*, by Lisa Randall, ©2011 Discover magazine.

61 P.38 *The Dancing Wu Li Masters*, Bantam Edition, by Gary Zukav © 1979

62 p. 26 Kybalion.

63 *From Science to God-the Mystery of Consciousness and the Meaning of Light*, ©2001 by Peter Russell

64 p.71-82 *The Non-Local Universe* by Nadean & Kafatos ©1999 Oxford University

65 p. 243 *Extraordinary Knowing* by Elizabeth Lloyd Mayer PhD ©2007

66 *The Physics of Consciousness* ©2000 by Evan Harris Walker PhD.

67 *The Physics of Consciousness*©2000 Evan Harris Walker, PhD

68 P. 308, *The Physics of Consciousness*©2000 Evan Harris Walker, PhD

69 P.1 *The Holographic Universe*, by Michael Talbot © 1991

70 *Mindful Universe: Quantum Mechanics and the Participating Observer* by Henry P. Stapp © 2007: Springer-Verlag

71 J. Ehrenwald, Telepathy and Medical Psychology ©1948 Norton, N.Y.

72 *New Worlds Beyond the Atom*. By Day L. (with DelaWarr G.). Republished by EP Publishing Limited, 1973; 95-96

73 Ibid.

74 *Investigation of the Fluctuation Dynamics of DNA Solutions by Laser Correlation Spectroscopy*. By Gariaev PP, Grigor'ev KV, Vasil'ev AA, Poponin VP, Shcheglov VA.Bulletin of the Lebedev Physics Institute, 1992:11-12; 23-30.

75 *Vacuum DNA phantom effect in vitro and its possible rational explanation*. By Gariaev PP, Poponin VP, Nanobiology 1995 (in press).

76 *Nature's Mind: The Quantum Hologram*, by Mitchell ED, International Journal of Computing *Anticipatory Systems*, Volume 7, *Fuzzy Systems, Genetic and Neural Algorithms, Quantum Neural Information Processing: New Technology ? New Biology ?* Partial Pro-

ceedings of the Third International Conference CASYS'99 on Computing Anticipatory Systems, Liège, Belgium, August 9-14, 1999, D. M. Dubois (Ed.), Publ. by CHAOS, pp. 295-312, 2000.

[77] *Miracles of Mind by Jane Katra*, PhD. And Russell Targ ©1998; *The Heart of the Mind* by Jane Katra, PhD. And Russell Targ ©1999;*Limitless Mind* by Russell Targ ©2004.

[78] *Extraordinary Knowing* by Elizabeth Lloyd Mayer, PhD. ©2007 Published Posthumously;

[79] *Psi Conducive States*, William G.Braud 1975, Journal of Communications 25 p-142-152

[80] *Extraordinary Knowing* by Elizabeth Lloyd Mayer, PhD. ©2007 Published Posthumously;

[81] Quoted from p.21, *My View of the World*, by Erwin Schrödinger, ©1964 Cambridge University Press, London

[82] Quoted from p.43-44 *The Phenomenon of Man*, by Teilhard de Chardin , © 1965 Harper Torchbooks,

[83] *Wholeness and the Implicate Order* ©1980 David Bohn.

END NOTES, CHAPTER 7 - THE WEIGHING OF THE HEART

[84] The coffin texts from the Nicropolis at Saqquara (2450 b.c.e.)

[85].

[86] St. Augustine, *Retractions*, Taken from P.54 *The Fathers of the Church, Saint Augustine, The Retractions*. Brogan c.1968 Catholic University of America Press. Augustine's Retractions were written as a clarification in 428 c.e., after publication of his seminal work the City of God in 427c.e.) *My own copy of St. Augustine's text, published by the Catholic University of America Press, caries the Nihil Obstat of John C. Selner, S.S., S.T.D. the Censor Librorum, and also the Imprimatur, of Patrick Cardinal A. O'Boyle, D.D. Archbishop of Washington. These are both official declarations that a book or pamphlet is FREE OF DOCTRINAL OR MORAL ERROR. No implication is contained therein that those who have granted the Nihil Obstat and Imprimatur agree with the contents, opinions or statements expressed. In laymen's terms, this means that the Catholic Church officially agree that these are the actual words of Saint Augustine himself, and they agree that he actually said, "That which is called the Christian Religion existed among the ancients, and never did Not exist, from the beginning of the human race". Saint Augustine clearly admits that paganism was in fact the Christian religion. Consequently, seeing the Roman emperor Justinian condemn paganism (Origenism) 120 years later illustrates that the emperors had no desire for true religion, only power and control. That original ancient religion St. Augustine identified as the true faith allowed for second chances without hellfire.*

[87] P. 226-227 "Justinian intervened in ecclesiastical matters more forcefully and systematically than any of his predecessors"…"With vigor he sought to wipe out the not inconsiderable remnants of paganism in the East"…"Backsliders into paganism were to be put to death"…."He even interfered to dictate Jewish doctrine forbidding teaching against the Last Judgment, resurrection of the dead and existence of angels. Rabbis were compelled to allow reading of the Bible in the synagogues in Greek or Latin along with Hebrew.….P. 246 Scholars are not agreed on how these anathemas became connected with the Council.….Some say the bishops gathered for the Council approved the anathameas presented tot hem by the emperor before the actual

opening of the official proceedings......At any rate they are continually linked to the work of the Council." *The First Seven Ecumenical Councils (325-787) Their History and Theology*©1983, Leo Donald Davis. *This is a great read and understanding the underlying regional differences in Christianity between Byzantium – Rome and Africa (Carthage-Alexandria) is very important in comprehending how the emperors played the factions against each other, and also that the doctrinal Christianity which has been handed down to us by this history, is indeed the watered down version which the Roman emperors needed to control the populace. Justinian did not murder "heretics" because he was a zealous Christian, it was instead because he was consolidating his power over his subjects*

[88] P.79, Old Souls, by Tom Shroder ©1999 Tom Shroder.

[89] Callanan & Kelley, 1992)

END NOTES, CHAPTER 8 – FACING DEATH

[90] Life after Life: by Raymond L. Moody Jr. M.D. ©1975, 1988 Bantam edition

[91] p. 150-151, *The French Revelation*, Edward C. Randall's Complete Works Compiled by N. Riley Heagerty ©1995

[92] *Parting Visions* ©1994 by Melvin Morse, M.D. with Paul Perry

[93] P. 10-12 *Coming Back to Life: The After Effects of the NDE* ©1988 by P.M.H. Atwater Ballantine Books

[94] ibid

[95] ibid

[96] P.14 *Coming Back to Life: The After Effects of the NDE* ©1988 by P.M.H. Atwater Ballantine Books

[97] Life after Life: by Raymond L. Moody Jr. M.D. ©1975, 1988 Bantam edition

[98] P.83-85 *Many Lives, Many Masters* © 1988 by Brian L. Weiss M.D.

[99] P.112 *Many Lives, Many Masters* © 1988 by Brian L. Weiss M.D.

[100] P.124 *Many Lives, Many Masters* © 1988 by Brian L. Weiss M.D.

END NOTES, CHAPTER 9 – BEGINNING THE JOURNEY

END NOTES, CHAPTER 10 - THE AFTERLIFE ROADMAP
NONE

END NOTES, CHAPTER 11 – CONTINUING AFTERLIFE
NONE

END NOTES, CHAPTER 12 – WHAT ALL THIS MEANS

[101] P.67, *Teachings of the Christian Mystics*, by Andrew Harvey ©1998

[102] Origen, *De Principis*

[103] P. 164, *The Field – Quest for the Secret Force of the Universe*, by Lynne McTaggart ©2008

[104] P.328 *Physics of Consciousness* © 2000 Evan Harris Walker

[105] p. 7-18, *Same Soul Many Bodies*, ©2004 By Brian L. Weiss, M.D.

[106] *The Perennial Philosophy* ©1945 by Aldous Huxley

[107] P. 176, *Why Religion Matters*, by Huston Smith ©2001 Harper-San Francisco

CPSIA information can be obtained at www.ICGtesting.com
Printed in the USA
LVOW042101160812

294530LV00001B/2/P